A-Z Street Atlas of WIRRAL

C000284335

Key to Maps

Reference

Motorway	M56
A Road	A57
Under Construction	
Proposed	
B Road	B5178
Dual Carriageway	
One Way A Roads	→
Traffic flow is indicated by a heavy line on the Drivers left.	
Pedestrianized Road	
Restricted Access	

Track or Footpath	=======
Residential Walkway	··········
Railway	Level Crossing / Station
Built Up Area	MILL / ST.
County Boundary	·+·+·
District Boundary	·—·—·
Posttown Boundary	
By arrangement with the Post Office	
Postcode Boundary	———
Within Posttown	
Map Continuation	10
Ambulance Station	✚

Church or Chapel	†
Fire Station	■
Hospital	Ⓗ
House Numbers	246 / 213
Selected Roads	
Information Centre	🛈
National Grid Reference	325
Police Station	▲
Post Office	★
Toilet	▽
With Facilities for the Disabled	♿

Scale

1:15,840
4 inches to 1 mile

| 0 | ¼ | ½ | ¾ Mile |
| 0 | 250 | 500 | 750 | 1 Kilometre |

Geographers' A-Z Map Co. Ltd.

Head Office : Fairfield Road, Borough Green, Sevenoaks, Kent TN15 8PP Telephone 01732 781000
Showrooms : 44 Gray's Inn Road, Holborn, London WC1X 8HX Telephone 0171-242-9246

4   32   395   94   93   92

A · B · C · D · E · F

1 · 2 · 3 · 3 · 4 · 5 · 6

RIVER MERSEY

Belfast 1.1 hours

Egremont

STREET

Alexandra Dock

Branch Dock (No.2)   33

Branch Dock (No.1)

LANGTON STREET

Branch Dock

Langton Dock

Dry Dock

BROCKLEBANK

Nth. Irish Ferries Ltd.

Branch Dock

Brocklebank Dock

Carriers Dock

Canada Branch Dock (No.3)

Canada Branch Dock (No.2)

Canada Dock

Canada Graving Dock

Canada Branch Dock (No.1)

Huskisson Branch Dock (No.3)

Huskisson Dock

Huskisson Branch Dock (No.1)

L 3

Sandon Half Tide Dock

Sandon Dock

Wellington Dock

Bramley Moore Dock

Nelson Dock

Salisbury Dock

Collingwood Dock

Stanley Dock

REGENT ROAD   A5036   A565

CHURCH ST.   DERBY

CHAPEL   Bootle Oriel Rd.

MILLERS   B

Works

RALEIGH ST.   DACRE ST.

DERBY ROAD

L20

BANKFIELD S.

Depot

Works

N   L I V

SANDHIL

DERBY STREET

L

BLACKSTONE ST.

Stanley Dock   HOWARD ST.   A565   GREAT

A · B · **12** · C · D

32   33

L I V

Egremont

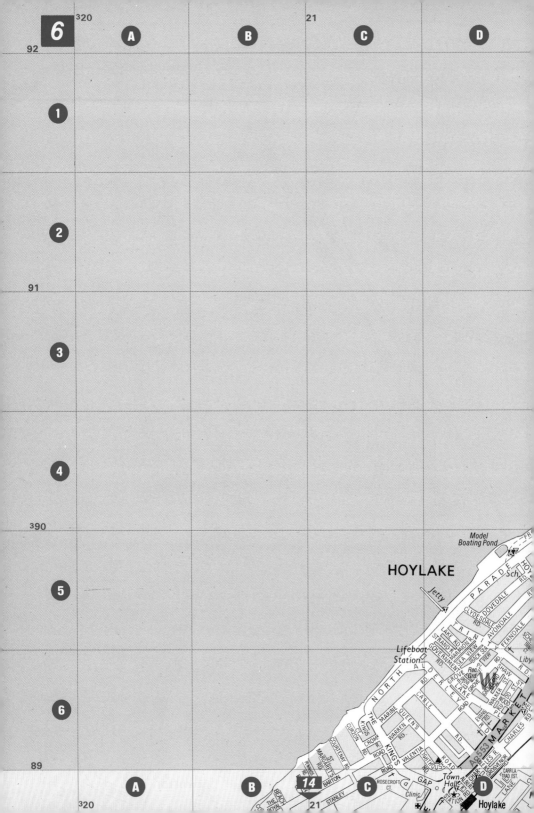

6

320

21

A   B   C   D

92

1

2

91

3

390

4

5

HOYLAKE

Model
Boating Pond

Jetty

6

Lifeboat
Station

89

A   B   14   C   D

320   21   Hoylake

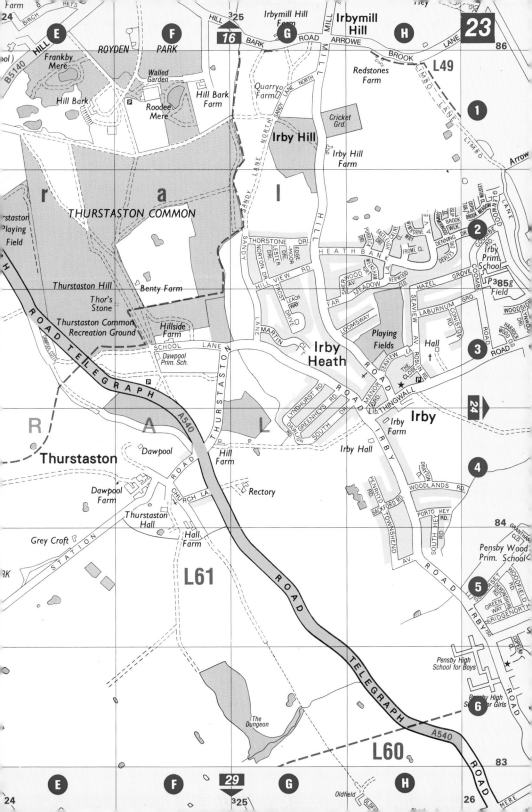

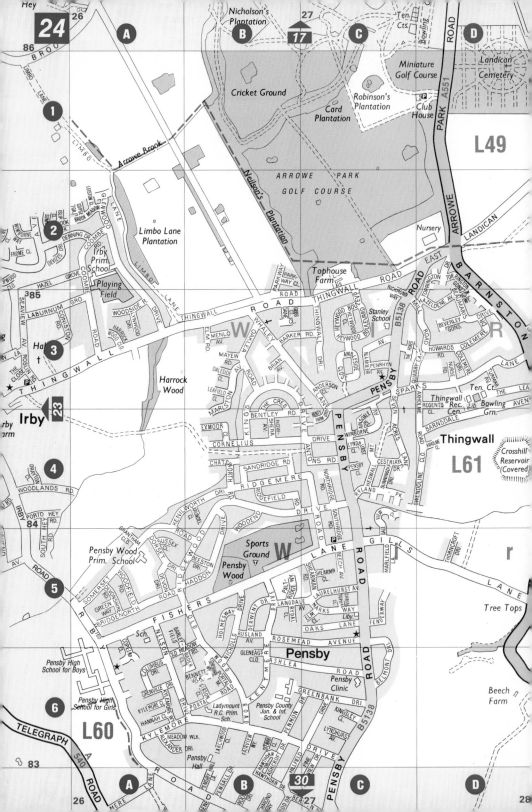

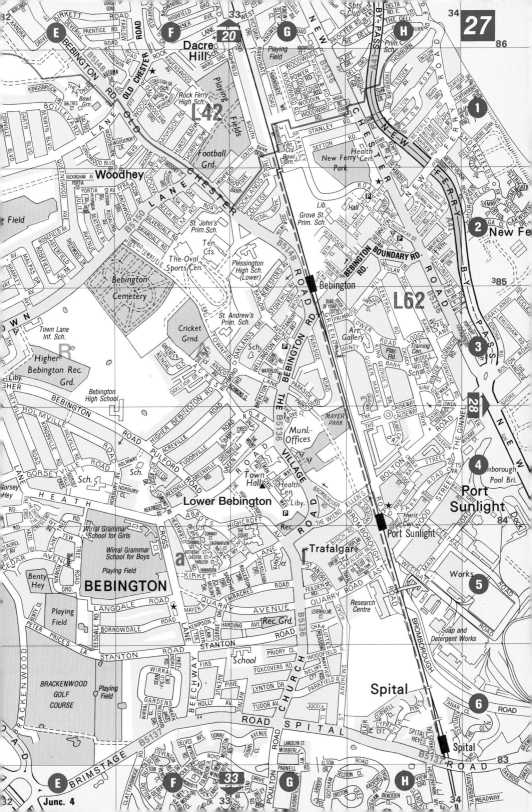

A B C D

31
▲26

Lower Underestone Cvert

1

Lady Farm
Iveston Farm
Home Farm
GREEN BNK
Tile Cottage

ROAD BRIMSTAGE ROAD A5137

Brimstage

Brook

CLATTERBRIDGE HOSPITAL & Sch.

2

Brooklet
The Brooklet
82

A5137

BRIMSTAGE

MANOR

TALBOT AVENUE

W   I   R

Clatterbridge Farm

Boat House

3

Manor House

Wirral Manor House

New Rocklands

▶ **31**
Pav.
Fish Ponds

ROAD CLATTERBRIDGE

Copley House

Westmead

GRANGE DR.

Croft Bank Cottages

Crofts Bank

COMMON THORNTON COMMON RD.
B5136

ROCKLANDS

Grange Farm

4

Hesketh Grange

Lodge

81

Hill Top Farm

Lodge

Strawberry Farm

ROAD

ST. GEORGE'S

MANOR

CHURCH RD.

THORNTON RD.

Thornton House

B5151

Pear Fa

Thornton Hough

SMITHY HL.

Play Fie

5

Lodge Farm

Pav.
Recreation Ground
Tele. Exchange

Allot. Gdns.

W   I   r

Raby Vale

THE

ROAD B5136

NESTON

ETON DRIVE
OXFORD DRIVE

▲

Nursery

Thornton Farm

Fish Pond

Chicken Cor Farm

WILLASTON

Sewage Works

Four Lanes End

WILLASTON B5151

6

WIDGEONS COVERT

Hotel

NESTON LANE

ROAD

MERE

White Cottage Farm

Westwood Farm
380
330

Pear Tree Farm

Hillyard Farm

THE GREEN

RO AD

37
▼31

Grange Farm

Raby

Westwood

A B C D

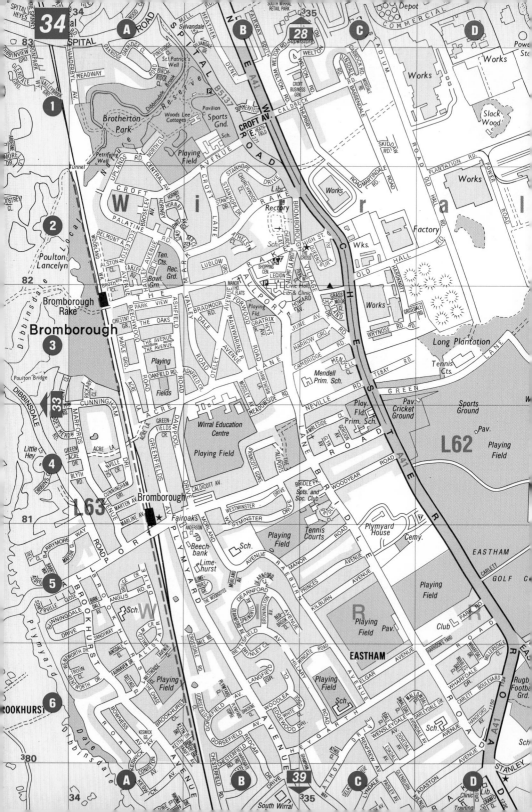

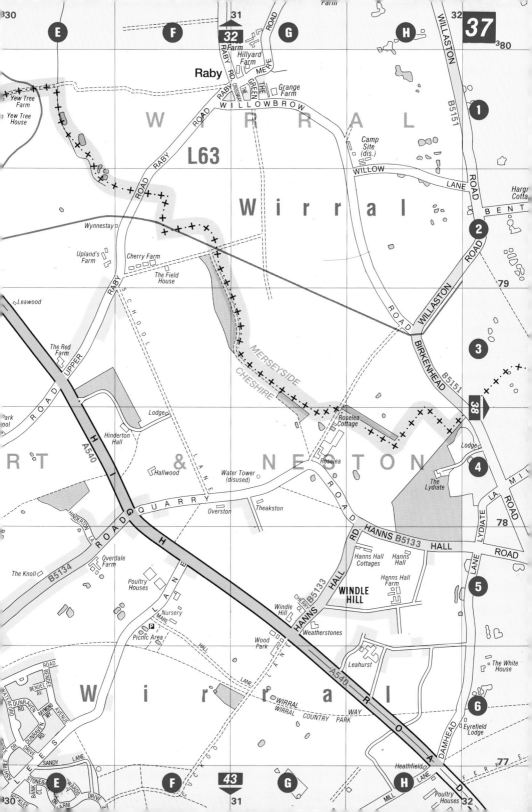

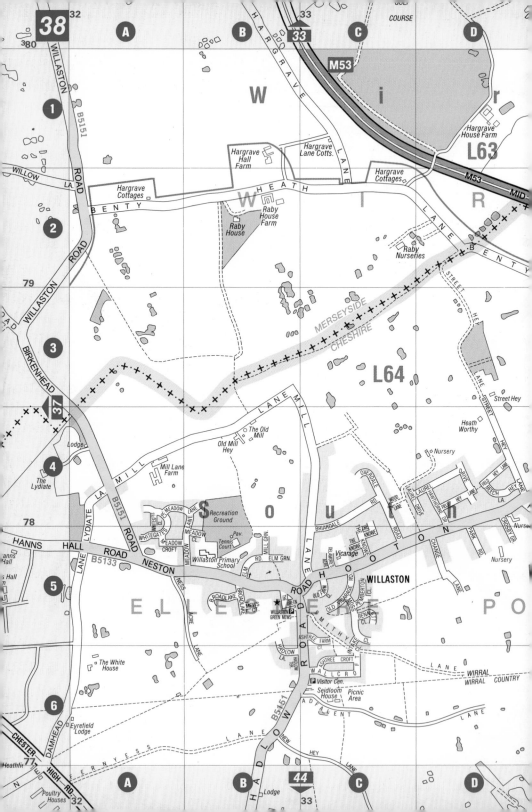

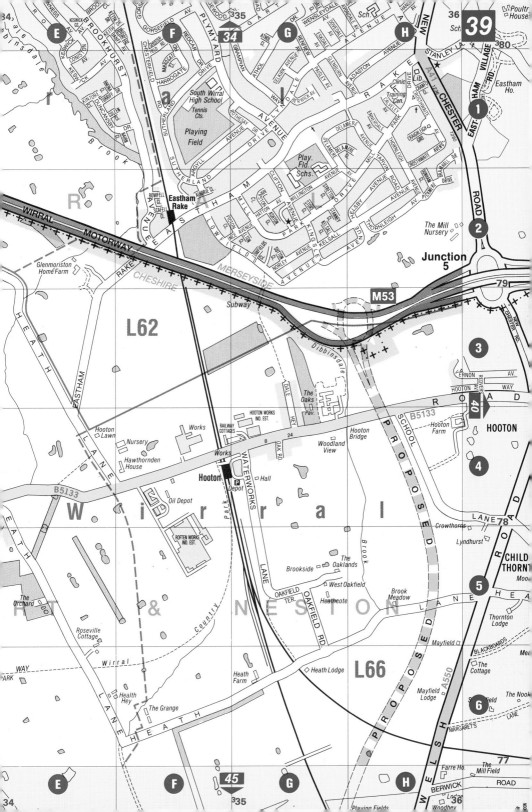

Grid/navigation references: E, F, 31, 37, G, H, CHESTER, 43, DAMHEAD, Evralfield, FERNY, 77, HIGH, ROAD, 1, 2, 76, 3, WOOD END LA, 44, 4, 375, 5, 6, 74, E, F, 31, G, 32, H, PUDDINGTON, LANE, 330

Place names and features:

330, DUBRAVEN RD, DRIVE, SANDY, LANE, CUCKOO, LANE, LEES, STONEBANK, BANK, CL, HOWARDS, WY, ROCKLEE, ROCK, FARM, GR, ROCK, FARM, CL, GUNSTONS, WOODFALL, Neston Junior School, WOODFALL, GR, CL, SCHOOL AV, SCHOOL, CL, CUMBERS DR, HOLT HEY, CUMBERS DR, W i r r a l, FLASHES LA, HILL TOP, HILL CL, VILL CL, Mill Farm, Heathfield, Poultry Houses, Ness Wood, Errington's Plantation, Poultry Houses, Haddon Hall Farm, NESS, MILL BANK, LABURNUM, FARM CL, PALACE HEY, SMITHS DRO, Pav, Playing Field, NESTON RD, L64, NESS GARDENS, Mickwell Brow, Orchard House, HADDON, Poultry Houses, Haddon Wood Poultry Farm, Haddon Hall Farm, HADDON, LANE, 76, Friends Hall, HADDON WOOD, Haddon Corner, Maybole, Elthorns Farm, Hillcrest, Red Bank Farm, Dunstan Farm, Dunst Woo, Nursery, Lodge, Chapel Cottages, DENHALL, Bracken, Locharwoods, WOOD LA, WOOD LANE, Hillmorto, Ryelands, R T & N E S T O N, Burton Point Station (disused), Station House, Mansard, Perrywood, Windmill (disused), Burton Wood, VICARAGE, Vicarage, PRIESTWAY, Wildflo, Green Acre, The Villa, MILL LANE, HADDON, ROAD, THE ROAD, RAKE, Hall, Recreation Ground, Tennis Cour, Peerswood Bungalows, Peer's Wood, Burton Point Farm, Hampson Well (disused), Manor Farm, Bath Wood, Burton, Church Farm, VILLAGE, DUMBAH, School, Burton Manor College, Barnacre, STATION RD, N E S S, DENHALL LANE

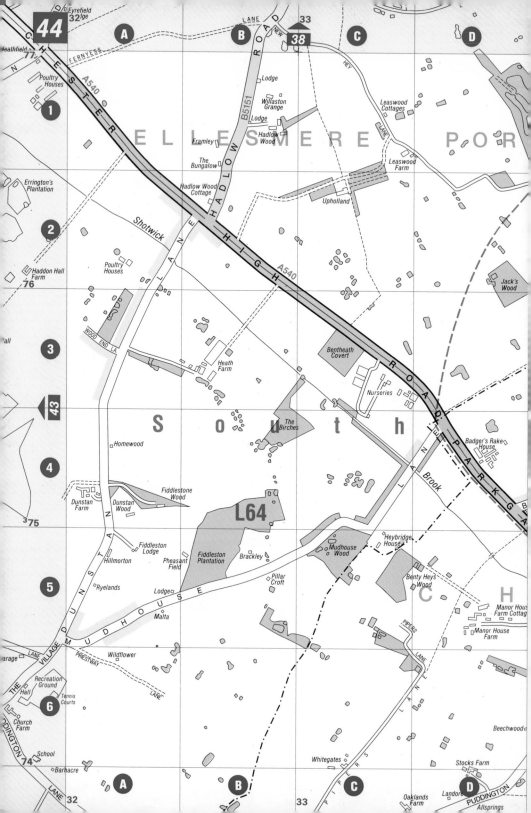

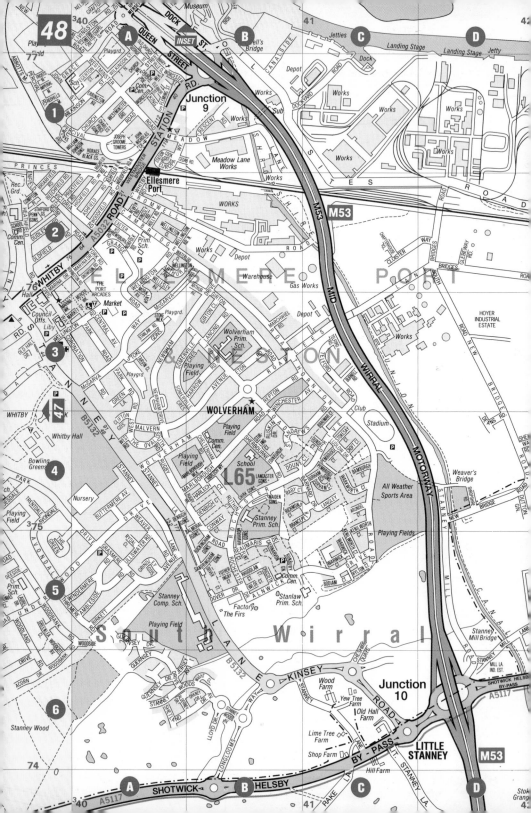

INDEX TO STREETS

HOW TO USE THIS INDEX

1. Each street name is followed by its Postal District and then by its map reference; e.g. Abbey Rd. L48 —5D **14** is in the Liverpool 48 Postal District and is to be found in square 5D on page **14**.
   The page number being shown in bold type.
   A strict alphabetical order is followed in which Av., Rd., St., etc. (though abbreviated) are read in full and as part of the street name; e.g. Ashcroft Dri. appears after Ash Clo. but before Ashdale Pk.

2. Streets and a selection of Subsidiary names not shown on the Maps, appear in the index in *Italics* with the thoroughfare to which it is connected shown in brackets;
   e.g. *Alexander Way. L8 —3H 21 (off Park Hill Rd.)*

3. With the now general usage of Postcodes for addressing mail, it is not recommended that this index is used for such a purpose.

GENERAL ABBREVIATIONS

All : Alley	Cen : Centre	Dri : Drive	Ind : Industrial	N : North	St : Street
App : Approach	Chu : Church	E : East	Junct : Junction	Pal : Palace	Ter : Terrace
Arc : Arcade	Chyd : Churchyard	Embkmt : Embankment	La : Lane	Pde : Parade	Up : Upper
Av : Avenue	Circ : Circle	Est : Estate	Lit : Little	Pk : Park	Vs : Villas
Bk : Back	Cir : Circus	Gdns : Gardens	Lwr : Lower	Pas : Passage	Wlk : Walk
Boulevd : Boulevard	Clo : Close	Ga : Gate	Mnr : Manor	Pl : Place	W : West
Bri : Bridge	Comn : Common	Gt : Great	Mans : Mansions	Rd : Road	Yd : Yard
B'way : Broadway	Cotts : Cottages	Grn : Green	Mkt : Market	S : South	
Bldgs : Buildings	Ct : Court	Gro : Grove	M : Mews	Sq : Square	
Bus : Business	Cres : Crescent	Ho : House	Mt : Mount	Sta : Station	

INDEX TO STREETS

Abbey Clo. L41 —2B **20**
Abbeyfield Ho. L66 —4G **47**
Abbey Rd. L48 —5D **14**
Abbey St. L41 —2B **20**
Abbot Clo. L43 —1A **18**
Abbots Dri. L63 —4F **27**
Abbotsford St. L44 —3A **12**
Abbots Way. L48 —4E **15**
Abbots Way. L64 —5C **36**
Abbotts M. L65 —1H **47**
Abercromby Sq. L7 —4H **13**
Aberdeen St. L41 —6G **11**
Aberford Av. L45 —6C **2**
Aber St. L6 —2H **13**
Abingdon Rd. L49 —4B **16**
Abram St. L5 —6G **5**
Acacia Clo. L49 —6C **16**
Acacia Dri. L66 —6F **47**
Acacia Gro. L44 —3A **12**
Acacia Gro. L48 —5C **14**
Ackers Rd. L49 —5A **18**
Acland Rd. L44 —1F **11**
Acorn Clo. L63 —3D **26**
Acorn Ct. L8 —1H **21**
Acorn Dri. L65 —6H **47**
Acrefield Ct. L42 —6F **19**
Acrefield Rd. L42 —6G **19**
Acre La. L60 —2E **31**
Acre La. L63 & L62 —4A **34**
(in two parts)
Acre Rd. L66 —2D **46**
Acres Rd. L47 —6H **7**
Acres Rd. L63 —3F **27**
Acreville Rd. L63 —4F **27**
Acton La. L46 —6C **8**
Acton Rd. L42 —6C **20**
Acuba Gro. L42 —3A **20**
Adam Av. L66 —5F **47**
(in two parts)
Adam Clo. L66 —3D **46**
Adam St. L5 —5H **5**
Adaston Av. L62 —1H **39**
Addington St. L44 —2H **11**
Addison St. L3 —2F **13**
Addison Way. L7 —3F **13**
Adelaide Pl. L5 —1G **13**
Adelaide Rd. L42 —3G **19**
Adelaide St. L44 —2F **11**
Adelphi St. L41 —1A **20**
Adfalent La. L64 —6C **38**
Adkins St. L5 —5H **5**
Adlington Ho. L3 —2F **13**
Adlington St. L3 —2F **13**
Admiral Gro. L8 —2H **21**
Admiral St. L8 —2H **21**
Agnes Gro. L44 —4G **3**
Agnes Rd. L42 —4A **20**
Aigburth Gro. L46 —5D **8**
Aiken Clo. L8 —3H **21**
Ailsa Rd. L45 —6E **3**

Ainsdale Clo. L61 —4C **24**
Ainsdale Clo. L63 —6A **34**
Ainsworth Av. L46 —1C **16**
Ainsworth St. L3 —4G **13**
Aintree Gro. L66 —4D **46**
Airdale Clo. L43 —1A **18**
Airdrie Clo. L62 —2F **39**
Aire Clo. L65 —6G **41**
Airlie Rd. L47 —1D **14**
Akbar, The. L60 —1G **29**
Alabama Way. L41 —1B **20**
Alastair Cres. L43 —6D **18**
Albany Gdns. L66 —6C **40**
Albany Rd. L42 —5A **20**
Albemarle Rd. L44 —2H **11**
Albert Dri. L44 —2H **11**
Albert Rd. L42 —3G **19**
Albert Rd. L47 —1D **14**
Albert Rd. L48 —6C **14**
Albert St. L65 —2G **3**
Albion Pl. L45 —3F **3**
Albion St. L5 —6G **5**
Albion St. L41 —1B **20**
Albion St. L45 —3E **3**
Aldams Gro. L4 —2G **5**
Alder Dri. L66 —6F **47**
Alderley Av. L41 —6D **10**
Alderley Rd. L44 —2F **11**
Alderley Rd. L47 —6D **6**
Alderney Clo. L65 —6A **48**
Alder Rd. L63 —5E **27**
Aldersgate. L42 —5B **20**
Aldersley Rd. L3 —2F **13**
Aldford Clo. L43 —5C **18**
Aldford Clo. L63 —5H **33**
Aldgate. L65 —2G **47**
Alexander Dri. L61 —6A **24**
Alexander Wlk. L4 —3H **5**
Alexander Way. L8 —3H 21
(off Park Hill Rd.)
Alexandra Ct. L45 —3E **3**
Alexandra Dri. L42 —6A **20**
Alexandra Dri. L63 —2G **19**
Alexandra Rd. L45 —3E **3**
Alexandra Rd. L48 —6C **14**
Alexandra St. L65 —2G **41**
Alfonso Rd. L4 —3F **5**
Alfred M. L1 —6G **13**
Alfred Pl. L8 —1H **21**
Alfred Rd. L43 —2G **19**
Alfred St. L44 —4A **12**
Alexandra Rd. L65 —2G **41**
Anglesea Way. L8 —3H **21**
Anglezark Rd. L44 —6F **3**
Angus Rd. L63 —5A **34**
Ann Clo. L66 —6D **40**
Annesley Rd. L44 —2G **11**
Anscot Av. L63 —3F **27**
Anson St. L3 —3H **13**
Anson Ter. L3 —3H **13**
Anstey Clo. L46 —4B **8**
Anthony's Way. L60 —4C **30**
Anthorn Clo. L43 —3B **18**
Antonio St. L20 —2F **5**
Antons Rd. L61 —4C **24**

Allonby Clo. L43 —3C **18**
Allport La. L62 —2B **34**
Allport La. Precinct. L62
—2B **34**
Allport Rd. L63 & L62 —5H **33**
Alma St. L41 —1A **20**
Alma St. L62 —2G **27**
Almond Pl. L46 —5F **9**
Almond Way. L49 —5C **16**
Alnwick Dri. L46 —5B **8**
Alnwick Dri. L65 —5B **48**
Alpha Dri. L42 —6C **20**
Alroy Rd. L4 —4H **5**
Alston Clo. L62 —2A **34**
Altcar Dri. L46 —6D **8**
Althorp St. L8 —4H **21**
Alton Rd. L43 —2E **19**
Alundale Ct. L20 —1E **5**
Alvanley Pl. L43 —1G **19**
Alvanley Rd. L66 —3E **47**
Alvanley Way. L66 —3E **47**
Alvega Clo. L62 —2A **28**
Alverstone Av. L41 —6D **10**
Alverstone Rd. L44 —2H **11**
Alvina La. L4 —4G **5**
Alwen St. L41 —4D **10**
Alwyn Gdns. L46 —5F **9**
Amberley Av. L46 —6C **8**
Amberley Clo. L46 —6C **8**
Ambleside Av. L46 —5D **8**
Ambleside Clo. L61 —3C **24**
Ambleside Clo. L62 —4C **34**
Ambleside Clo. L65 —5A **48**
Amelia Clo. L6 —2H **13**
Amery Gro. L42 —5G **19**
Amity St. L8 —2H **21**
Anchorage, The. L64 —6A **36**
Anderson Clo. L61 —3C **24**
Anderson Ct. L63 —5A **34**
Anderson St. L5 —5G **5**
(in two parts)
Andrew St. L4 —2H **5**
Andrew's Wlk. L60 —3D **30**
Anfield Rd. L4 —4H **5**

Antrim Dri. L66 —5F **47**
Anzacs, The. L62 —3A **28**
Appin Rd. L41 —2A **20**
Appledale Dri. L66 —6B **46**
Apple Garth. L46 —1C **16**
Appleton Dri. L49 —4E **17**
Appleton Clo. L65 —4F **47**
Appletree Gro. L66 —6A **46**
Apsley Av. L45 —5F **3**
Apsley Rd. L62 —1H **27**
Arborn Dri. L49 —1G **17**
Arcade, The. L65 —2G **47**
Archbishop Wlk. L3 —1E **13**
Archer Clo. L4 —4F **5**
Archers Ct. L49 —5G 17
(off Childwall Grn.)
Archer St. L4 —4F **5**
Archers Way. L49 —5G **17**
Archers Way. L66 —6E **47**
Arden Dri. L64 —1C **42**
Arderne Clo. L63 —1H **33**
Argos Pl. L20 —2F **5**
Argos Rd. L20 —2F **5**
Argyle Rd. L4 —5F **3**
Argyle St. L41 —1A **20**
Argyle St. S. L41 —2A **20**
Argyll Av. L62 —1F **39**
Arkle Rd. L43 —5D **10**
Arkwood Clo. L62 —6A **28**
Arkwright St. L5 —6G **5**
Arley Clo. L43 —1A **18**
Arley St. L3 —1E **13**
Arlington Ct. L43 —2D **18**
Arlington Rd. L45 —5C **2**
Armthorpe Dri. L66 —2B **46**
Arno Ct. L43 —4F **19**
Arnold Clo. L8 —1H **21**
Arnold St. L8 —1H **21**
Arnold St. L45 —6F **3**
Arno Rd. L43 —4F **19**
Arnot St. L4 —2H **5**
Arnot Way. L63 —3D **26**
Arnside Rd. L43 —3E **19**
Arnside Rd. L45 —6F **3**
Arrad St. L7 —5H **13**
Arrowe Av. L46 —6D **8**
Arrowe Brook La. L49 —1D **16**
Arrowe Brook Rd. L49 —5F **17**
Arrowe Ct. L49 —5G 17
(off Childwall Grn.)
Arrowe Pk. Rd. L49 —2G **17**
Arrowe Rd. L49 —4D **16**
Arrowe Side. L49 —3E **17**
Arthur Av. L65 —2A **48**
Arthur St. L41 —6G **11**
(in two parts)
Arundel Av. L45 —5D **2**
Arundel Clo. L61 —4A **20**
Arundel Clo. L46 —4C **48**
Arundel St. L4 —2G **5**

Asbury Rd. L45 —5B **2**
Ascot Dri. L63 —4F **27**
Ascot Dri. L66 —4D **46**
Ascot Gro. L63 —4F **27**
Ashbourne Clo. L66 —6A **46**
Ashbrook Ter. L63 —3G **27**
Ashburton Av. L43 —1D **18**
Ashburton Rd. L43 —1D **18**
Ashburton Rd. L44 —1F **11**
Ashburton Rd. L48 —4D **14**
Ashby Clo. L46 —4B **8**
Ash Clo. L66 —6F **47**
Ashcroft Dri. L61 —1B **30**
Ashdale Pk. L49 —5C **16**
Ashdown Dri. L49 —5C **16**
Ashfield Cres. L62 —3B **34**
Ashfield Rd. L62 —3A **34**
Ashfield Rd. L65 —2A **48**
Ashfield Rd. N. L65 —2A **48**
Ashfield St. L5 —6E **5**
Ash Gro. L4 —3H **5**
Ash Gro. L45 —4G **3**
Ash Gro. L66 —1C **46**
Ashlea Rd. L61 —6B **24**
Ashley Av. L47 —4H **7**
Ashley St. L42 —5B **20**
Ashmore Clo. L48 —3A **22**
Ash Rd. L42 —3H **19**
Ash Rd. L63 —2F **27**
Ashton Clo. L62 —2G **39**
Ashton Dri. L48 —6C **14**
Ashton St. L3 —3H **13**
Ashtree Clo. L64 —6E **37**
Ashtree Croft. L64 —6C **38**
Ashtree Dri. L64 —1E **43**
Ashtree Farm Ct. L64 —5C **38**
Ash Vs. L44 —3G **11**
Ashville Rd. L43 & L41 —1E **19**
Ashville Rd. L44 —3G **11**
Ash Way. L60 —5D **30**
Ashwell St. L8 —6G **13**
Ashwood Clo. L66 —6D **46**
Ashwood Ct. L43 —4H **9**
Askew St. L44 —1H **11**
Askew St. L4 —5F **3**
Askrigg Av. L66 —2B **46**
Aspen Clo. L60 —4F **31**
Aspen Clo. L66 —6F **47**
Aspendale Rd. L42 —3H **19**
Aspinall St. L5 —4F **5**
Aspinall St. L41 —6G **11**
Asquith Av. L41 —6F **11**
Asterfield Av. L63 —2E **27**
Aston Clo. L43 —4D **18**
Astonwood Rd. L42 —4H **19**
Astor St. L4 —2H **5**
Athelstan Clo. L62 —2B **34**
Atherton Clo. L5 —6G **5**

Atherton Ct. L45 —3E **3**
Atherton Dri. L49 —4G **17**
Atherton Rd. L65 —1F **47**
Atherton St. L45 —2E **3**
Athol Bri. L5 —6E **5**
Athol Clo. L62 —1G **39**
Athol St. L62 —1G **39**
Athol St. L5 —6D **4**
(in two parts)
Athol St. L41 —6A **12**
Atlantic Pavilion. L3 —5E **13**
Atlantic Way. L3 —2F **21**
Atterbury St. L8 —2G **21**
Attwood St. L4 —4H **5**
Atwell St. L6 —1H **13**
Atworth Ter. L64 —5B **38**
(off Neston Rd.)
Aubrey Ct. L6 —1H **13**
Aubrey St. L6 —1H **13**
(in two parts)
Auburn Rd. L45 —4E **3**
Aubynes, The. L45 —4C **2**
Auckery Av. L66 —4D **46**
Audlem Av. L43 —4D **18**
Audley St. L3 —3G **13**
Aughton Clo. L49 —2G **17**
Austin St. L4 —3E **11**
Autumn Gro. L42 —1E **27**
Avelon Clo. L43 —2B **18**
Avenue, The. L62 —3A **34**
Avon Clo. L4 —3G **5**
Avon Clo. L64 —1C **42**
Avondale. L65 —4H **47**
Avondale Av. L46 —4F **9**
Avondale Av. L62 —6C **34**
Avondale Av. L47 —5D **6**
Avon St. L41 —4D **10**
Axholm Clo. L61 —4D **24**
Axholme Clo. L61 —4D **24**
Axholme Rd. L61 —3D **24**
Axholm Rd. L61 —3D **24**
Aylesbury Av. L43 —5C **18**
Aylesbury Clo. L66 —4G **43**
Aylesbury Rd. L45 —4G **3**
Aylsham Dri. L49 —6G **9**
Aysgarth Rd. L45 —5D **2**

Bk. Barlow La. L4 —3G **5**
Bk. Bedford St. N. L7 —4H **13**
Bk. Bedford St. S. L7 —5H **13**
Bk. Berry St. L1 —6G **13**
Bk. Blackfield Ter. L4 —4F **5**
Bk. Bold St. L1 —1G **13**
Bk. Boundary St. L5 —5F **5**
Bk. Bridport St. L3 —3G **13**
Bk. Canning St. L8 —5H **13**
Bk. Catharine St. L8 —5H **13**
Bk. Chadwick Mt. L5 —4G **5**
Bk. Colquitt St. L1 —1G **13**

A-Z Wirral 49

Braemar Ct. L65 —4C 48
Braemar St. L20 —2F 5
Braemore Rd. L44 —1D 10
Braeside Clo. L66 —2C 46
Braeside Gdns. L49 —2F 17
Braid St. L41 —5H 11
Bramble Av. L41 —5D 10
Bramble Way. L46 —3D 8
Bramerton Ct. L48 —4C 14
Bramford Clo. L49 —2E 17
Bramhall Dri. L62 —2H 39
Bramley Av. L63 —2E 27
Bramley Clo. L66 —6A 46
Brampton Dri. L8 —5H 13
Brampton St. L8 —5H 13
Bramwell Av. L43 —6E 19
Brancepeth Ct. L65 —4B 48
Brancote Gdns. L62 —4B 34
Brancote Mt. L43 —1D 18
Brancote Rd. L43 —1D 18
Brandon St. L41 —1B 20
Bran St. L8 —2G 21
Brasenose Rd. L20 —1D 4
Brassey St. L8 —1G 21
Brassey St. L41 —5E 11
Brattan Rd. L41 —3G 19
Braunton Rd. L45 —5E 3
Bray St. L41 —5F 11
Breck Clo. L6 —6H 5
Breckfield Pl. L5 —6H 5
Breckfield Rd. N. L5 —5H 5
Breck Pl. L44 —2E 11
Breck Rd. L5 —1H 13
Breck Rd. L44 —1D 10
Breckside Av. L44 —1C 10
Breck, The. L66 —6E 41
Breck Wlk. L6 —1H 13
Brecon Dri. L66 —6E 47
Brecon Rd. L42 —6G 19
Bredon Clo. L66 —1A 46
Breeze Hill. L20 & L9 —1F 5
Breezehill Clo. L64 —5C 36
Breezehill Pk. L64 —5D 36
Breezehill Rd. L64 —5D 36
Breeze La. L9 —1H 5
Brenig St. L41 —4D 10
Brentwood Ct. L49 —5G 17
(off Childwall Grn.)
Brentwood St. L44 —3G 11
Brereton Av. L63 —3G 27
Brett St. L41 —5F 11
Brewster St. L4 & L20 —2G 5
Brian Av. L61 —3B 24
Briardale Gdns. L66 —1C 46
Briardale Rd. L42 —3G 19
Briardale Rd. L44 —3A 12
Briardale Rd. L63 —2F 27
Briardale Rd. L64 —4C 38
Briardale Rd. L66 —1C 46
Briar Dri. L60 —3C 30
Briarfield Rd. L60 —3C 30
Briarfield Rd. L65 —2H 47
Briar St. L4 —4F 5
Briarswood Clo. L42 —1F 27
Brick St. L1 —6F 13
Bride St. L4 —1H 5
Bridge Ct. L48 —4C 14
Bridge Ct. L64 —6C 36
Bridgecroft Rd. L45 —5F 3
Bridge Farm Clo. L49 —3H 17
Bridge Meadow. L66 —5F 47
Bridgenorth Rd. L61 —5A 24
Bridge Rd. L48 —4C 14
Bridges Rd. L65 —2D 48
Bridge St. L20 —1D 4
Bridge St. L41 —6A 12
Bridge St. L62 —4H 27
(in two parts)
Bridge St. L64 —6C 36
Bridgewater St. L1 —6F 13
Bridge Wood Dri. L66 —5C 46
Bridle Av. L44 —3A 12
Bridle Clo. L43 —1H 17
Bridle Clo. L62 —4C 34
Bridle Pk. L62 —4C 34
Bridle Rd. L44 —3A 12
Bridle Rd. L62 —4C 34
Bridle Way. L66 —4D 46
Bridport St. L3 —3G 13
Briedden Way. L66 —1A 46
Brighton St. L44 —1H 11
Bright St. L6 —2H 13
Bright St. L41 —1G 19
(in two parts)
Bright Ter. L8 —4H 21
Brightwell Clo. L49 —3F 17
Brill St. L41 —5F 11
Brimstage Av. L63 —1D 26
Brimstage Clo. L60 —4E 31
Brimstage Grn. L60 —3F 31
Brimstage La. L63 —5B 26
Brimstage Rd. L4 —1G 5
Brimstage Rd. L60 & L63 —4E 31
Brimstage St. L41 —3G 19
Brindley St. L8 —1F 21
Brinley Clo. L62 —6B 34
Brisbane Av. L45 —3E 3
Briscoe Av. L46 —6E 9
Briscoe Dri. L46 —6E 9
Bristol Av. L44 —1G 11
Bristol Dri. L66 —6E 47
Britannia Cres. L8 —4H 21
Britannia Pavilion. L3 —5E 13
Britannia Rd. L45 —1E 11
Britton St. L8 —6F 13
Broadbelt St. L4 —1H 5
Broadfield Av. L43 —6A 10
Broadfield Clo. L43 —6H 9
Broadlake. L64 —5B 38
Broadland Gdns. L66 —5F 47
Broadland Rd. L66 —5F 47
Broad La. L60 —2G 29
Broadmead. L60 —4E 31
Broadoaks. L49 —1E 17
Broadstone Dri. L63 —1F 33
Broadway. L45 —6D 2
Broadway. L49 —2E 17
Broadway. L63 —2D 26
Broadway Av. L45 —6D 2
Brocklebank St. L20 —1C 4
Brockley Av. L45 —2F 3
Brockmoor Tower. L4 —3F 5
Brock St. L4 —3F 5
Bromborough Dock Est. L62 —3B 28
Bromborough Rd. L63 —4G 27
Bromborough Village Rd. L62 —2B 34
Brome Way. L63 —1H 33
Bromley Clo. L60 —4A 30
Bromley Rd. L45 —4E 3
Brompton Av. L44 —1G 11
Brompton Way. L66 —6E 47
Bromsgrove Rd. L49 —3C 16
Bronington Av. L62 —5B 34
Bronte St. L3 —3G 13
Brook Clo. L44 —6G 3
Brookdale Av. N. L49 —3E 17
Brookdale Av. S. L49 —3E 17
Brookdale Clo. L49 —3E 17
Brookfield Gdns. L48 —5D 14
Brookfield Rd. L48 —5D 14
Brook Hey. L64 —3A 36
Brookhurst Av. L63 & L62 —5A 34
Brookhurst Clo. L63 —6A 34
Brookhurst Rd. L63 —5A 34
Brookland Rd. L41 —2H 19
Brooklands. L41 —6H 11
Brooklands Gdns. L64 —4A 36
Brooklands Rd. L64 —4A 36
Brook La. L64 —3A 36
Brooklet Rd. L60 —3E 31
Brooklyn Dri. L65 —2F 47
Brook Meadow. L61 —2A 24
Brook Rd. L66 —2D 46
Brooks All. L1 —4F 13
Brookside Cres. L49 —2D 16
Brookside Dri. L49 —2E 17
Brook St. L3 —3D 12
Brook St. L41 —5G 11
Brook St. L62 —3G 27
Brook St. L64 —5C 36
Brook St. E. L41 —6A 12
Brook Ter. L48 —5D 14
Brook Wlk. L61 —2H 23
Brookway. L43 —6C 18
Brookway. L45 —6E 3
Brookway. L49 —2E 17
Brook Well. L64 —2C 42
Broomfield Clo. L60 —2G 29
Broom Hill. L43 —6D 10
Broomlands. L60 —3A 30
Broseley Av. L62 —2A 34
Broster Av. L46 —5C 8
Broster Clo. L46 —5C 8
Brosters La. L47 —4F 7
Brotherton Clo. L62 —3A 34
Brotherton Rd. L44 —3A 12
Brougham Av. L41 —4B 20
Brougham Rd. L44 —2H 11
Brougham Ter. L6 —2H 13
Broughton Av. L48 —4C 14
Broughton Rd. L44 —2F 11
Brow La. L60 —4B 30
Browning Av. L42 —6B 20
Browning Dri. L65 —3F 47
Browning Grn. L65 —3F 47
Browning Rd. L45 —6B 2
Brownlow Hill. L3 —4G 13
Brownlow Rd. L62 —2H 27
Brownlow St. L3 —4H 13
Brow Rd. L43 —4B 10
Brow Side. L5 —1H 13
Broxton Av. L43 —5D 18
Broxton Av. L48 —4E 15
Broxton Rd. L45 —5D 2
Broxton Rd. L66 —2E 47
Bruce Cres. L63 —5A 34
Bruce Dri. L66 —3C 46
Bruce St. L8 —3H 21
Bruera Rd. L65 —3F 47
Brunel Clo. L6 —1H 13
Brunel M. L6 —1H 13
Brunel Wlk. L6 —6H 5
Brunsfield Clo. L46 —6C 8
Brunstath Clo. L60 —2E 31
Brunswick Bus. Pk. L3 —3F 21
Brunswick Clo. L4 —3G 5
Brunswick Ct. L41 —6A 12
Brunswick Cres. L66 —4E 47
Brunswick Pl. L20 —3D 4
Brunswick Rd. L6 —2H 13
Brunswick St. L2 —4E 13
Brunswick St. L3 —4D 12
Brunswick Way. L3 —2F 21
Bryanston Rd. L42 —5E 19
Bryn Bank. L44 —1G 11
Brynford Heights. L5 —6G 5
Brynmoss Av. L44 —1D 10
Bryony Way. L42 —1F 27
Buccleuch St. L41 —4D 10
Buchanan Rd. L9 —1H 5
Buchanan Rd. L44 —2H 11
Buckingham Av. L43 —6D 10
Buckingham Av. L63 —2E 27
Buckingham Gdns. L65 —5B 48
Buckingham Rd. L44 —1D 10
Buckingham St. L5 —6G 5
Buckland Dri. L63 —1F 33
Bude Clo. L43 —1A 18
Budworth Clo. L43 —3C 18
Budworth Rd. L43 —3C 18
Budworth Rd. L66 —5E 47
Buerton Clo. L43 —3C 18
Buffs La. L60 —2D 30
Buggen La. L64 —5B 36
Buildwas Rd. L64 —3C 36
Bulkeley Rd. L44 —2H 11
Bullens Rd. L4 —3H 5
Bull Hill. L64 —1D 42
Bulrushes, The. L17 —4H 21
Bulwer St. L42 —5B 20
Bunbury Grn. L65 —5B 48
Burbo Way. L45 —3C 2
Burden Rd. L46 —4C 8
Burdett Av. L63 —1G 33
Burdett Clo. L63 —1G 33
Burdett Rd. L45 —6B 2
Burdett Rd. L66 —5E 47
Burford Av. L44 —2D 10
Burgess St. L3 —3G 13
Burleigh M. L5 —4H 5
Burleigh Rd. N. L5 —4H 5
Burleigh Rd. S. L5 —5H 5
Burlingham Av. L48 —6F 15
Burlington Rd. L45 —2F 3
Burlington St. L3 —1E 13
Burlington St. L41 —1A 20
Burnaby St. L44 —1H 11
Burnand St. L4 —4H 5
Burnell Rd. L65 —3C 48
Burnley Av. L46 —5F 9
Burnley Ct. L6 —1H 13
Burnley Rd. L46 —4F 9
Burns Av. L45 —6E 3
Burns Clo. L66 —3E 47
Burnside Av. L44 —3F 11
Burnside Rd. L44 —3F 11
Burrell Clo. L42 —6G 19
Burrell Ct. L42 —6G 19
Burrell Dri. L46 —6D 8
Burrell Rd. L42 —1C 26
Burrell St. L4 —3H 5
Burroughs Gdns. L3 —1F 13
Burrows Ct. L3 —6E 5
Burton Av. L45 —6C 2
Burton Grn. L66 —3D 46
Burton Rd. L64 —6C 36
Burton St. L5 —5D 4
Busby's Cotts. L45 —3F 3
Bushell Clo. L64 —6D 36
Bushell Rd. L64 —6D 36
Bush Way. L60 —3A 30
Bute St. L5 —1G 13
(in two parts)
Butterfield St. L4 —4H 5
Buttermere Av. L43 —1A 18
Buttermere Av. L65 —4A 48
Butterton Av. L49 —1D 16
Button St. L2 —4E 13
Buxton La. L44 —6C 2
Buxton Rd. L42 —5C 20
Byerley St. L44 —3A 12
Byles St. L8 —3H 21
Byng St. L20 —1D 4
Byrne Av. L42 —6B 20
Byrom St. L3 —2F 13
Byrom Way. L3 —2F 13
Byron Clo. L43 —1H 25

Cable Rd. L47 —6C 6
Cable Rd. S. L47 —1D 14
Cable St. L1 —4E 13
Cadmus Wlk. L6 —1H 13
Caernarvon Clo. L49 —1G 17
Caernarvon Ct. L63 —5F 27
Caernarvon Ct. L65 —5B 48
Caerwys Gro. L42 —3A 20
Caird St. L6 —2H 13
Cairo St. L4 —2G 5
Caithness Dri. L45 —5G 3
Caithness Gdns. L43 —6D 18
Caldbeck Rd. L62 —1B 34
Calder Av. L43 —5E 19
Calder Rd. L5 —5H 5
Calder Rd. L63 —4D 26
Calder St. L5 —5G 5
Calder Way. L66 —2C 46
Caldicott Av. L62 —4B 34
Caldwell Dri. L49 —5H 17
Caldy Chase Dri. L48 —2B 22
Caldy Ct. L48 —6D 14
Caldy Dri. L66 —3D 46
Caldy Grange Clo. L48 —6F 15
Caldy Rd. L45 —6F 3
Caldy Rd. L48 —6D 14
Caldy Wood. L48 —2B 22
Caledonia St. L7 —5H 13
Callaghan Clo. L5 —6F 5
Calne Clo. L61 —2H 23
Calveley Av. L62 —1H 39
Calveley Clo. L43 —4D 18
Cambrian Clo. L46 —6B 8
Cambrian Clo. L66 —1A 46
Cambrian Rd. L46 —6C 8
Cambridge Rd. L20 —1F 5
Cambridge Rd. L42 —5F 19
Cambridge Rd. L45 —4F 3
Cambridge Rd. L62 —3B 34
Cambridge Rd. L65 —2A 48
Cambridge St. L7 —4H 13
(in two parts)
Camden Rd. L65 —2G 47
Camden St. L3 —3G 13
Camden St. L41 —1A 20
Cameron Rd. L46 —2H 9
Cammell Ct. L43 —1F 19
Campbell St. L1 —5F 13
Campbeltown Rd. L41 —2B 20
Camperdown St. L41 —1B 20
Canal Ct. L65 —1G 41
Canalside. L65 —1B 48
Canalside Gro. L5 —6E 5
Canal St. L20 —1D 4
Candia Tower. L5 —5G 5
Candlish Pl. L6 —6H 5
Canning Pl. L1 —4E 13
(in two parts)
Canning St. L8 —5H 13
Canning St. L41 —6A 12
Cannock Clo. L66 —6A 46
Cannon Hill. L43 —1F 19
Cannon Mt. L43 —1F 19
Cannon St. L65 —2G 47
Canterbury Clo. L66 —6A 46
Canterbury Rd. L42 —6C 20
Canterbury Rd. L44 —2G 11
Canterbury St. L3 —2G 13
Canterbury Way. L3 —2G 13
Capenhurst La. L65 —4F 47
Carden Clo. L4 —4G 5
Cardiff Clo. L66 —6A 46
Cardigan Av. L41 —1H 19
Cardigan Rd. L45 —4F 3
Cardus Clo. L46 —5B 8
Carey Av. L63 —3D 26
Cargill Gro. L42 —1H 27
Carham Rd. L47 —1E 15
Carisbrooke Clo. L48 —1A 22
Carisbrooke Rd. L20 & L4 —1G 5
Carlaw Rd. L42 —5E 19
Carlett Boulevd. L62 —6D 34
Carlett Pk. L62 —5D 34
Carlisle Clo. L43 —2G 19
Carlisle M. L43 —2G 19
Carlton Clo. L64 —3A 36
Carlton Cres. L66 —5F 41
Carlton La. L47 —5E 7
Carlton Mt. L42 —4A 20
Carlton Rd. L42 —3G 19
Carlton Rd. L45 —3F 3
Carlton Rd. L63 —5H 27
Carlton St. L3 —1D 12
Carlton Ter. L47 —5E 7
Carlyle Cres. L66 —3E 47
Carmarthen Cres. L8 —1F 21
Carmel Clo. L45 —3F 3
Carmel St. L5 —5G 5
Carmichael Av. L49 —5D 16
Carnforth Clo. L41 —2G 19
Carnoustie Clo. L46 —4B 8
Carnsdale Rd. L46 —5F 9
Carol Dri. L60 —3E 31
Caroline Pl. L43 —2F 19
Carpenter's La. L48 —5D 14
Carr Bri. Rd. L49 —3H 17
Carr Ga. L46 —5B 8
Carr Hey. L46 —5B 8
Carr Hey Clo. L49 —5A 18
Carr Ho. La. L46 —5B 8
Carrick Dri. L65 —5H 47
Carrington Rd. L45 —5G 3
Carrington St. L41 —5E 11
Carr La. L47 & L46 —4H 7
(Great Meols)
Carr La. L47 —1D 14
(Hoylake)
Carr La. L48 —2F 15
Carr La. Trading Est. L47 —1D 14
Carrock Rd. L62 —1C 34
Carrow Clo. L46 —5B 8
Carruthers St. L3 —2E 13
Carsgoe Rd. L47 —1E 15
Carsthorne Rd. L47 —1E 15
Carters, The. L49 —3C 16
Carter St. L8 —6H 13
Carterton Rd. L47 —1E 15
Cartmel Clo. L41 —2G 19
Cartmel Dri. L46 —6E 9
Cartmel Dri. L66 —5F 47
Carver St. L3 —2H 13
Caryl Gro. L8 —3G 21
Caryl St. L8 —1F 21
(in three parts)
Cases St. L1 —4F 13
Cassio St. L20 —1G 5
Castle Clo. L46 —2G 9
Castle Dri. L60 —3B 30
Castle Dri. L65 —4G 47
Castle Fields Est. L46 —1F 9
Castleford Rise. L46 —2E 9
Castlegrange Clo. L46 —1E 9
Castleheath Clo. L46 —2E 9
Castle Mt. L60 —3B 30
Castle Rd. L45 —5E 3
Castle St. L2 —4E 13
Castle St. L41 —1B 20
Castleway N. L46 —1G 9
Castleway S. L46 —2G 9
Catharine St. L8 —6H 13
Cathcart St. L41 —6H 11
Cathedral Clo. L1 —6G 13
Cathedral Ga. L1 —5G 13
Cathedral Wlk. L3 —4G 13
Catherine St. L41 —1H 19
Caulfield Dri. L49 —4E 17
Causeway Clo. L62 —3H 27
Causeway, The. L62 —3H 27
(in two parts)
Cavell Dri. L65 —3G 47
Cavendish Dri. L42 —6H 19
Cavendish Gdns. L65 —3G 47
Cavendish Ho. L4 —2G 5
Cavendish Rd. L41 —6F 11
Cavendish Rd. L45 —2F 3
Cavendish St. L41 —5F 11
Cavern Walks. L2 —4E 13
Cavour Ho. L5 —1G 13
Cawood Clo. L66 —2B 46
Caxton Clo. L43 —1A 18
Caxton Clo. L66 —3F 47
Cazeneau St. L3 —1F 13
Cearn's Rd. L43 —2E 19
Cecil Rd. L42 —5F 19
Cecil Rd. L44 —1E 11
Cecil Rd. L45 —1E 11
Cecil Rd. L62 —1H 27
Cedab Rd. L65 —1A 48
Cedar Av. L63 —5E 27
Cedar Av. L66 —1C 46
Cedardale Dri. L66 —6A 46
Cedar Gro. L64 —5D 36
Cedars, The. L46 —6C 8
Cedar St. L41 —2H 19
Cedarway. L60 —6D 30
Cedarwood Clo. L49 —3C 16
Celia St. L20 —2F 5
Celtic Rd. L47 —4G 7
Celtic St. L8 —1H 21
Central Av. L62 —2A 34
Central Av. L65 —3A 48
Central Pk. Av. L44 —1G 11
Central Rd. L62 —2H 27
(New Ferry)
Central Rd. L62 —5H 27
(Port Sunlight)
Central Shopping Cen. L1 —4F 13
Centurion Clo. L47 —4G 7
Centurion Dri. L47 —4G 7
Ceres Ct. L43 —6A 10
Ceres St. L20 —2E 5
Cestrian Dri. L61 —4C 24
Chadwick St. L3 —1D 12
Chadwick St. L46 —5E 9
Chalfield Av. L66 —2C 46
Chalfield Clo. L66 —2C 46

Chalkwell Dri. L60 —3E **31**
Challis St. L41 —4C **10**
Chaloner St. L1 —6F **13**
Chamberlain St. L41 —3B **20**
Chamberlain St. L44 —3E **11**
Chancel St. L4 —4F **5**
Change La. L64 —5D **38**
Channel, The. L45 —3C **2**
Chantrell Rd. L48 —5G **15**
Chantry Clo. L43 —1A **18**
Chantry Wlk. L60 —5C **30**
Chapel Clo. L65 —2G **41**
Chapel Gdns. L5 —6F **5**
Chapelhill Rd. L46 —5F **9**
Chapel M. L65 —3H **47**
Chapel Rd. L47 —5E **7**
Chapel St. L3 —3D **12**
Chapel Ter. L20 —1D **4**
Chapman Clo. L8 —2G **21**
Chapterhouse Clo. L65 —2C **48**
Charing Cross. L41 —1H **19**
Charlcombe St. L42 —3H **19**
Charlecote St. L8 —4H **21**
Charles Price Gdns. L65 —1A **48**
Charles Rd. L47 —1D **14**
(in three parts)
Charles St. L41 —6H **11**
Charlesville. L43 —2F **19**
Charlesville Ct. L43 —2F **19**
Charlotte Rd. L44 —6H **3**
Charlotte's Meadow. L63 —5G **27**
Charlotte Way. L1 —4F 13
(off St John's Precinct)
Charlton Ct. L43 —1D **18**
Charlwood Clo. L43 —1A **18**
Charter Cres. L66 —4E **47**
Charter Ho. L44 —1H **11**
Chase Dri. L66 —5E **47**
Chase, The. L63 —6A **34**
Chase Way. L5 —1G **13**
Chase Way. L66 —5E **47**
Chatburn Wlk. L8 —3H **21**
Chatham Rd. L42 —5C **20**
Chatham St. L7 —5H **13**
Chatsworth Av. L44 —1G **11**
Chatsworth Clo. L66 —2D **46**
Chatsworth Rd. L42 —5C **20**
Chatsworth Rd. L61 —4B **24**
Chaucer St. L3 —2F **13**
Cheapside. L2 —3E **13**
Cheapside All. L2 —3E 13
(off Cheapside)
Chelmsford Clo. L4 —4F **5**
Cheltenham Rd. L45 —5C **2**
Cheltenham Rd. L65 —4B **48**
Chenotrie Gdns. L43 —2B **18**
Chepstow Av. L44 —1G **11**
Chepstow St. L4 —2G **5**
Cheriton Av. L48 —5F **15**
Cherrybank. L44 —3F **11**
Cherry Brow Ter. L64 —5B 38
(off Green, The)
Cherry Clo. L64 —5G **37**
Cherry Gro. L66 —6G **47**
Cherry Sq. L44 —1F **11**
Cherrytree Rd. L46 —5F **9**
Cheshire Acre. L49 —5G **17**
Cheshire Gro. L46 —6E **9**
Cheshire Quays. L65 —6C **48**
Cheshire Way. L61 —6B **24**
Chesnut Gro. L42 —3H **19**
Chester Ct. L63 —5F **27**
Chesterfield Rd. L62 —6B **34**
Chesterfield St. L8 —6G **13**
Chester High Rd. L64 & L66 —6F **31**
Chester Rd. L60 —4D **30**
Chester Rd. L64 —6C **36**
Chester Rd. L66 —4A **40**
(Childer Thornton)
Chester Rd. L66 & L65 —6B **46**
(Whitbyheath)
Chester St. L8 —6G **13**
Chester St. L41 —2B **20**
Chester St. L44 —2E **11**
Chestnut Av. L66 —6F **47**
Chestnut Clo. L49 —6C **16**
Chestnut Gro. L62 —3A **34**
Cheswood Ct. L49 —6G 17
(off Childwall Grn.)
Chetwynd Clo. L43 —3D **18**
Chetwynd Rd. L43 —2E **19**
Cheverton Clo. L49 —4H **17**
Cheviot Clo. L42 —6H **19**
Cheviot Clo. L66 —1A **46**
Cheviot Rd. L42 —6G **19**
Chidden Clo. L49 —4C **16**
Childer Cres. L66 —6B **40**
Childer Gdns. L66 —6B **40**
Childwall Av. L46 —6D **8**
Childwall Clo. L46 —6D **8**
Childwall Ct. L66 —5F **41**
Childwall Gdns. L66 —5F **41**
Childwall Grn. L49 —5G **17**
Childwall Rd. L66 —5F **41**
Chillingham St. L8 —4H **21**
Chiltern Rd. L42 —6G **19**
Chilton Dri. L66 —5E **47**
China Farm La. L48 —3G **15**
Chippenham Av. L49 —3C **16**
Chirkdale St. L4 —2G **5**
Chirk Gdns. L65 —4B **48**
Chirk Way. L46 —6F **9**
Chisenhale St. L3 —1E **13**
Cholmondeley Rd. L48 —5D **14**
Cholmondeley Rd. L65 —3F **47**
Cholsey Clo. L49 —3F **17**
Chorley Way. L63 —2G **33**
Chorlton Gro. L45 —6B **2**
Christchurch Rd. L43 —3F **19**
Christian St. L3 —2F **13**
Christie Clo. L66 —3A **40**
Christleton Clo. L43 —5B **18**
Christleton Dri. L66 —1E **47**
Christmas St. L20 —2F **5**
Christopher Dri. L62 —6E **35**
Christophers Clo. L61 —5C **24**
Christopher St. L4 —3H **5**
Church All. L1 —4F **13**
Church Clo. L44 —1H **11**
Church Cres. L44 —3A **12**
Church Dri. L62 —3H **27**
Church Farm Ct. L60 —4B **30**
Church Gdns. L44 —1H **11**
Church Hill. L44 —6D **2**
Church Hill. L45 —6D **2**
Churchill Av. L41 —6F **11**
Churchill Ct. L64 —5C **36**
Churchill Gro. L44 —6G **3**
Churchill Way. L64 —5C **36**
Churchill Way N. L3 —3F **13**
Churchill Way S. L3 —3F **13**
Churchlands. L44 —3A 12
(off Bridle Rd.)
Church La. L4 —1H **5**
Church La. L44 —1H **11**
Church La. L49 —5H **17**
Church La. L61 —4F **23**
Church La. L62 —2B **34**
Church La. L64 —6C **36**
Church La. L66 —3D **46**
Churchmeadow Clo. L44 —1H **11**
Church Meadow La. L60 —4A **30**
Church Pde. L65 —1A **48**
Church Pl. L42 —4H **19**
Church Rd. L4 —1H **5**
Church Rd. L42 —4H **19**
Church Rd. L44 —3A **12**
Church Rd. L48 —6C **14**
Church Rd. L49 —2A **18**
Church Rd. L63 —6G **27**
(Bebington)
Church Rd. L63 —5B **32**
(Thornton Hough)
Church Rd. W. L4 —1H **5**
Church St. L1 —4F **13**
Church St. L20 —1C **4**
Church St. L41 —1B **20**
Church St. L44 —1H **11**
Church St. L65 —1A **48**
Church Ter. L42 —4H **19**
Churchview Rd. L41 —5F **11**
Church Wlk. L20 —1D **4**
Church Wlk. L48 —6D **14**
Church Wlk. L65 —1A **48**
Churchwood Clo. L62 —2B **34**
Churchwood Ct. L49 —6H **17**
Churnet St. L4 —3G **5**
Churn Way. L49 —3D **16**
Churton Av. L43 —4D **18**
Churton Ct. L6 —2H **13**
Circular Dri. L49 —4D **16**
Circular Dri. L60 —2B **30**
Circular Dri. L62 —2H **27**
Circular Rd. L41 —2H **19**
Cirencester Av. L49 —3C **16**
Citrine Rd. L44 —3H **11**
City Rd. L4 —2H **5**
Civic Way. L1 —3F **13**
Civic Way. L63 —4G **27**
Civic Way. L65 —2H **47**
Clare Cres. L44 —6D **2**
Clare Dri. L65 —5H **47**
Claremont Dri. L63 —5F **27**
Claremont Rd. L48 —4D **14**
Claremont Way. L63 —1D **26**
Claremount Dri. L63 —5F **27**
Claremount Rd. L45 & L44 —4D **2**
Clarence Rd. L42 —4G **19**
Clarence Rd. L44 —3H **11**
Clarence St. L3 —4G **13**
Clarendon Clo. L43 —2G **19**
Clarendon Rd. L44 —2H **11**
Clarendon Wlk. L43 —2G **19**
Clare Rd. L20 —1F **5**
Clare Ter. L5 —5G **5**
Clare Way. L45 —6D **2**
Claribel St. L8 —1H **21**
Clarke Av. L42 —5A **20**
Clatterbridge Rd. L63 —4D **32**
(in two parts)
Claughton Dri. L44 —2F **11**
Claughton Firs. L43 —3F **19**
Claughton Grn. L43 —2F **19**
Claughton Pl. L41 —1G **19**
Claughton Rd. L41 —1G **19**
Clayfield Clo. L20 —1F **5**
Clayhill Grn. L66 —6C **40**
Clayhill Ind. Pk. L64 —3D **36**
Clay St. L3 —1D **12**
Clayton Ct. L44 —3E **11**
Clayton La. L44 —3E **11**
Clayton Pl. L41 —2G **19**
Clayton Sq. L1 —4F **13**
Clayton St. L41 —2G **19**
Clee Hill Rd. L42 —6G **19**
Clegg St. L5 —1G **13**
Clement Gdns. L3 —1E **13**
(in two parts)
Cleopas St. L8 —3H **21**
Clevedon St. L8 —2H **21**
Cleveland Dri. L66 —1A **46**
Cleveland Sq. L1 —5F **13**
Cleveland St. L41 —5F **11**
Cleveley Rd. L47 —5G **7**
Cliff Dri. L44 —6H **3**
Cliffe Rd. L64 —2D **42**
Clifford Rd. L44 —2F **11**
Clifford St. L41 —5E **11**
Cliff Rd. L44 —2D **10**
Cliff, The. L45 —2D **2**
Clifton Av. L62 —2G **39**
Clifton Cres. L41 —1A **20**
Clifton Gdns. L65 —4A **48**
Clifton Gro. L44 —1H **11**
Clifton Rd. L41 —2H **19**
Clifton St. L3 —3G **13**
Clipper View. L62 —1H **27**
Clive Rd. L41 —3G **19**
Clive Rd. L43 —3G **19**
Cloister Way. L65 —2C **48**
Closeburn Av. L60 —5A **30**
Close, The. L42 —6H **19**
Close, The. L49 —5D **16**
Close, The. L61 —3H **23**
Close, The. L63 —6H **19**
Cloverfield Gdns. L66 —6D **40**
Clwyd Dri. L66 —1A **46**
Clwyd St. L41 —1H **19**
(in two parts)
Clwyd St. L45 —4E **3**
Clydesdale. L65 —4H **47**
Clydesdale Rd. L44 —6H **3**
Clydesdale Rd. L47 —5D **6**
Clyde St. L20 —3E **5**
Clyde St. L42 —5B **20**
Coalbrookdale Rd. L64 —3D **36**
Coal St. L3 —3G **13**
Coastal Dri. L45 —3B **2**
Coastguard La. L64 —4A **36**
Cobden Av. L42 —4B **20**
Cobden Ct. L42 —4B **20**
Cobden Pl. L42 —4B **20**
Cobden St. L6 —2H **13**
Cobham Rd. L46 —6D **8**
Coburg St. L41 —1H **19**
Coburg Wharf. L3 —1E **21**
Cochrane St. L5 —6H **5**
Cockburn St. L8 —3H **21**
Cockerell Clo. L4 —4H **5**
Cockspur St. L3 —3E **13**
Cockspur St. W. L3 —3E **13**
Cokers, The. L42 —1E **27**
Coldstream Dri. L66 —2H **45**
Coleman Dri. L49 —4C **16**
Colemere Ct. L65 —6H **41**
Colemere Dri. L61 —3D **24**
Cole St. L43 —1G **19**
College Clo. L43 —1H **17**
College Clo. L45 —5C **2**
College Dri. L63 —2G **27**
College La. L1 —4F **13**
College St. N. L6 —2H **13**
College St. S. L6 —2H **13**
College View. L20 —1E **5**
Colliery Grn. Clo. L64 —2C **42**
Colliery Grn. Ct. L64 —2C **42**
Colliery Grn. Dri. L64 —2C **42**
Collingham Grn. L66 —2B **46**
Collingwood Rd. L63 —5H **27**
Collin Rd. L43 —5C **10**
Colmore Av. L63 —2F **33**
Colonnades, The. L3 —5D **12**
Colquitt St. L1 —5G **13**
Columbia La. L43 —3F **19**
Columbia Rd. L4 —1H **5**
Columbia Rd. L43 —3F **19**
Columbus Dri. L61 —6A **24**
Columbus Quay. L3 —4G **21**
Column Rd. L48 —5E **15**
Colville Rd. L44 —1E **11**
Colwyn St. L41 —5D **10**
Comely Av. L44 —1G **11**
Comely Bank Rd. L44 —1H **11**
Commercial Rd. L5 —5E **5**
Commercial Rd. L62 —6C **28**
Common Field Rd. L49 —6H **17**
Commutation Row. L3 —3F **13**
Compass Ct. L45 —3D **2**
Compton Pl. L65 —2H **47**
Compton Rd. L41 —4B **10**
Comus St. L3 —2F **13**
Concert St. L1 —4F **13**
Concordia Av. L49 —2G **17**
Concourse Ho. L1 —3F **13**
Concourse, The. L48 —4C **14**
Coney Wlk. L49 —1D **16**
Conifer Clo. L66 —6B **46**
Coningsby Dri. L45 —1E **11**
Coningsby Rd. L4 —4H **5**
Coniston Av. L43 —2A **18**
Coniston Av. L45 —4C **2**
Coniston Av. L63 —1E **39**
Coniston Clo. L66 —3B **40**
Coniston Rd. L61 —3H **23**
Coniston Rd. L64 —1C **42**
Connaught Clo. L41 —5E **11**
Connaught Way. L41 —5D **10**
Constance St. L3 —3H **13**
Constantine Av. L60 —2C **30**
Convent Clo. L42 —3H **19**
Conville Boulevd. L63 —1E **27**
Conway Clo. L63 —4D **26**
Conway Ct. L41 —1H **19**
Conway Ct. L63 —5F **27**
Conway Ct. L65 —4B **48**
Conway Pl. L41 —1A **20**
Conway St. L5 —6G **5**
Conway St. L41 —6G **11**
Cook Rd. L46 —1H **9**
Cookson St. L1 —6G **13**
Cook St. L2 —4E **13**
Cook St. L41 —2H **19**
Cook St. L65 —1A **48**
Coombe Pk. L66 —1C **46**
Coombe Pk. Ct. L66 —1C **46**
Coombe Rd. L61 —2A **24**
Cooperage Clo. L8 —3G **21**
Copeland Clo. L61 —5A **24**
Copperas Hill. L3 —4G **13**
Copperfield Clo. L8 —2H **21**
Coppice Clo. L43 —1H **17**
Coppice Grange. L46 —6C **8**
Coppice Gro. L49 —5C **16**
Coppice, The. L45 —4E **3**
Coppice, The. L66 —6A **46**
Copse Gro. L61 —2A **24**
Coral Ridge. L43 —1B **18**
Corbyn St. L44 —4A **12**
Corfu St. L41 —1G **19**
Corinthian St. L42 —5B **20**
Corinth Tower. L5 —5G **5**
Corinto St. L8 —6G **13**
Cornelius Dri. L61 —4B **24**
Cornfield Clo. L66 —6F **47**
Corn Hill. L1 —5E **13**
Corniche Rd. L62 —3H **27**
Corn St. L8 —2G **21**
Cornwall Clo. L62 —1H **27**
Cornwall Ct. L63 —5F **27**
Cornwall Dri. L43 —6E **19**
Cornwallis St. L1 —5F **13**
Corona Rd. L62 —3A **28**
Coronation Av. L45 —4F **3**
Coronation Bldgs. L45 —1F **11**
Coronation Dri. L62 —6B **28**
Coronation Rd. L47 —1B **14**
Coronation Rd. L65 —3H **47**
Corporation Rd. L41 —5D **10**
Corrie Dri. L63 —5F **27**
Cortsway. L49 —2E **17**
Cortsway W. L49 —2D **16**
Corwen Clo. L43 —1H **17**
Corwen Clo. L46 —6F **9**
Corwen Rd. L47 —6E **7**
Costain St. L20 —3E **5**
Cotswold Rd. L42 —6G **19**
Cottage Clo. L63 —6A **34**
Cottage Clo. L64 —6C **36**
Cottage Dri. E. L60 —6B **30**
Cottage Dri. W. L60 —6B **30**
Cottage La. L60 —6B **30**
Cottage St. L41 —6H **11**
Cottesmore Dri. L60 —3F **31**
Cotton St. L3 —1D **12**
Cottonwood. L17 —4H **21**
Coulsdon Pl. L8 —3H **21**
Coulthard Rd. L42 —1G **27**
County Rd. L4 —2H **5**
Courtenay Rd. L47 —6C **6**
Courtney Av. L44 —2E **11**
Courtney Rd. L42 —1G **27**
Court, The. L63 —5G **27**
Court, The. L64 —1D **42**
Covent Garden. L2 —3D **12**
Coventry Av. L66 —6A **46**
Coventry St. L41 —1H **19**
Covertside. L48 —5F **15**
Cowan Way. L6 —1H **13**
Cowdrey Av. L43 —4A **10**
Cow La. L66 —1C **46**
Cowley Clo. L49 —2D **16**
Cowley Rd. L4 —2H **5**
Craig Gdns. L66 —6E **41**
Craigleigh Gro. L62 —1H **39**
Cranbourne Av. L41 —6D **10**
Cranbourne Av. L46 —6D **8**
Cranbourne Av. L47 —4G **7**
Cranford Clo. L62 —1H **39**
Cranford St. L44 —3G **11**
Cranmer St. L5 —6E **5**
Cranswick Grn. L66 —2C **46**
Cranwell Rd. L49 —4B **16**
Craven Clo. L41 —1H **19**
Craven Pl. L41 —6G **11**
Craven St. L3 —3G **13**
Craven St. L41 —1G **19**
Creek, The. L45 —3C **2**
Creer St. L5 —1G **13**
Crescent Rd. L44 —1G **11**
Crescent Rd. L65 —1B **48**
Crescent, The. L48 —5C **14**
Crescent, The. L49 —4D **16**
Crescent, The. L61 —3B **24**
Crescent, The. L63 —4E **27**
Crescent, The. L65 —2F **47**
Cressida Av. L63 —2E **27**
Cressingham Rd. L45 —3F **3**
Cressington Av. L42 —6H **19**
Cressington Gdns. L65 —1A **48**
Cresson Ct. L43 —2D **18**
Cresswell St. L6 —1H **13**
Crete Tower. L5 —5G **5**
Crewe Grn. L49 —5G **17**
Criccieth Ct. L65 —5B **48**
Crifton Clo. L66 —5C **46**
Crocus Av. L41 —5D **10**
Crocus St. L5 —4F **5**
Croesmere Dri. L66 —5D **46**
Croft Av. L62 —2A **34**
Croft Av. E. L62 —1B **34**
Croft Bus. Cen. L62 —1B **34**
Croft Clo. L43 —3C **18**
Croft Cotts. L66 —5A **40**
Croft Ct. L65 —4C **48**
Croft Dri. L46 —6E **9**
Croft Dri. L48 —3A **22**
Croft Dri. E. L48 —2B **22**
Croft Dri. W. L48 —2A **22**
Croft Edge. L43 —4F **19**
Croften Dri. L64 —2C **42**
Crofters Clo. L66 —6E **47**
Crofters Heath. L66 —6E **47**
Crofters, The. L49 —3D **16**
Croft La. L62 —2B **34**
Crofton Rd. L42 —4A **20**
Croftsway. L60 —3H **29**
Croft, The. L49 —5D **16**
Cromarty Rd. L44 —1D **10**
Cromer Dri. L45 —6E **3**
Cromer Rd. L47 —6C **6**
Crompton St. L5 —6F **5**
Cromwell Rd. L4 —1G **5**
Cromwell Rd. L65 —2A **48**
Cronton Av. L46 —2E **9**
Croome Dri. L48 —5E **15**
Cropper St. L1 —4F **13**
Crosby Clo. L49 —1F **17**
Crosby Gro. L64 —4D **38**
Crosfield Rd. L44 —2G **11**
Crossdale Rd. L62 —5B **34**
Crosshall St. L1 —3F **13**
Cross Hey Av. L43 —2B **18**
Cross La. L45 —6B **2**
Cross La. L63 —5F **27**
Cross La. L64 —2C **42**
Crossley Av. L66 —1E **47**
Crossley Dri. L60 —3H **29**
Cross St. L41 —1B **20**
Cross St. L62 —4H **27**
Cross St. L64 —5C **36**
Cross, The. L62 —2C **34**
Cross, The. L64 —6C **36**
Crossway. L43 —5C **10**
Crossways. L62 —6B **28**
Crossway, The. L63 —1G **37**
Crosthwaite Av. L62 —1H **39**
Croston Ct. L2 —3E **13**
Croughton Ct. L66 —5F **41**
Croughton Rd. L66 —5F **41**
Crowmarsh Clo. L49 —3F **17**
Crown St. L7 —3H **13**
Crow St. L8 —1F **21**
Croxteth Av. L44 —1F **11**
Croylands St. L4 —3G **5**
Crump St. L1 —6G **13**
Crutchley Av. L41 —5F **11**
Cubbin Cres. L5 —5F **5**

Elton Dri. L63 —6G 27
Elton St. L4 —1H 5
Elwyn Rd. L47 —3G 7
Elwy St. L8 —2H 21
Ely Av. L46 —5C 8
Ely Clo. L66 —6A 46
Emerald St. L8 —4H 21
Emerson St. L8 —6H 13
Emery St. L4 —2H 5
Empress Rd. L44 —1G 11
Emslie Ct. L64 —6A 36
Enerby Clo. L43 —6A 10
Enfield Rd. L65 —2H 47
Enfield Ter. L43 —2F 19
Enid St. L8 —1H 21
Ennerdale Av. L62 —1H 39
Ennerdale Rd. L43 —6C 18
Ennerdale Rd. L45 —3D 2
Ennerdale St. L3 —1F 13
Ennisdale Dri. L48 —4F 15
Ensor St. L20 —2D 4
Epping Ct. L60 —2C 30
Epworth Grange. L43 —1E 19
Epworth St. L6 —3H 13
Erfurt Av. L63 —5G 27
Erica Ct. L60 —2A 30
Eric Gro. L44 —1E 11
Eric Rd. L44 —1E 11
Eridge St. L8 —4H 21
Ermine Cres. L5 —6H 5
Errington Av. L65 —1A 48
Errington St. L5 —5D 4
Erskine Ind. Est. L6 —2H 13
Erskine Rd. L44 —2G 11
Erskine St. L6 —2H 13
Escolme Dri. L49 —4D 16
Esher Clo. L43 —6A 10
Esher Clo. L62 —1H 27
Esher Rd. L62 —1H 27
Eskdale. L65 —4H 47
Eskdale Av. L46 —4C 8
Eskdale Av. L62 —6C 34
Esk St. L20 —2D 4
Espin St. L4 —2H 5
Esplanade. L42 —5C 20
Essex Rd. L48 —4E 15
Essex St. L8 —2H 21
Ethelbert Rd. L47 —5E 7
Ethel Rd. L44 —2H 11
Etna St. L42 —5B 20
Eton Dri. L63 —5H 31
Eton Rd. L65 —3B 48
Eton St. L4 —2H 5
Europa Boulevd. L41 —1A 20
Europa Way. L65 —1A 48
Euston Gro. L43 —2G 19
Euston St. L4 —1H 5
Evans Rd. L47 —6D 6
Evelyn Rd. L44 —2G 11
Evelyn St. L5 —5F 5
Everest Clo. L66 —4F 47
Everest Rd. L42 —5H 19
Evergreen Clo. L49 —1E 17
Everleigh Clo. L43 —6H 9
Eversleigh Dri. L63 —5G 27
Eversley Pk. L43 —4F 19
Eversley St. L8 —1H 21
Everton Brow. L3 —2G 13
Everton Rd. L6 —1H 13
Everton Valley. L4 —4G 5
Everton View. L20 —1D 4
Evesham Rd. L45 —5D 2
Ewloe Ct. L65 —5B 48
Exchange Pas. E. L2 —3E 13
Exchange Pas. W. L2 —3E 13
Exchange St. E. L2 —3E 13
Exeter Rd. L20 —1E 5
Exeter Rd. L44 —6G 3
Exeter Rd. L65 —2A 48
Exmoor Clo. L61 —4B 24
Exmouth Gdns. L41 —1H 19
Exmouth St. L41 —1H 19
Exmouth Way. L41 —1H 19

Fairacres Rd. L63 —5G 27
Fairbeech Ct. L43 —6A 10
Fairbeech M. L43 —6A 10
Fairclough La. L43 —3F 19
Fairclough St. L1 —4F 13
Fairfax Rd. L41 —3A 20
Fairfield Av. L65 —5G 47
Fairfield Cres. L46 —5D 8
Fairfield Dri. L48 —4G 15
Fairfield Rd. L42 —5A 20
Fairhaven Clo. L42 —5B 20
Fairhaven Dri. L63 —6A 34
Fairholme Av. L64 —4B 36
Fairlawn Clo. L63 —5G 33
Fairleaf Way. L43 —6A 10
Fairmead Rd. L46 —4E 9
Fairoak Clo. L43 —6A 10
Fairoak M. L43 —6A 10
Fairtree Clo. L43 —6A 10
Fair View. L41 —3A 20
Fairview Av. L45 —6E 3
Fairview Clo. L43 —4F 19
Fair View Pl. L8 —3H 21
Fairview Rd. L43 —5F 19
Fairview Rd. L65 —5G 47
Fairview Way. L61 —6B 24
Fairway Cres. L62 —5B 28
Fairway N. L62 —5B 28
Fairways Dri. L66 —5D 40
Fairway S. L62 —6B 28
Falcongate Ind. Est. L44 —4G 11
(off Old Gorsey La.)
Falcon Rd. L41 —3G 19
Falcon Rd. L66 —4F 47
Falkland Rd. L44 —2H 11
Falkland St. L3 —3H 13
(in two parts)
Falkland St. L41 —5E 11
Falkner Pl. L8 —5H 13
Falkner Sq. L8 —5H 13
Fallowfield Rd. L46 —5G 9
Falstaff St. L20 —2E 5
Faraday Rd. L65 —3G 47
Faraday St. L5 —6H 5
Farley Av. L62 —2A 34
Farlow Rd. L42 —6B 20
Farm Clo. L49 —3C 16
Far Meadow La. L61 —3G 23
Farmers Heath. L66 —5D 46
Farmfield Dri. L43 —6A 10
Farmside. L46 —2F 9
Farmstead Way. L66 —6E 47
Farndon Av. L45 —5C 2
Farndon Dri. L48 —4G 15
Farndon Rd. L66 —1E 47
Farndon Way. L43 —3D 18
Farnworth Av. L46 —1E 9
Farr Hall Dri. L60 —4A 30
Farr Hall Rd. L60 —3A 30
Farriers Way. L48 —5B 16
Faulkner St. L8 —5H 13
Faulkner Ter. L8 —5H 13
Fazakerley St. L3 —3D 12
Fearnley Hall. L41 —2H 19
Fearnley Rd. L41 —2H 19
Feather La. L60 —3B 30
Feilden Rd. L63 —5G 27
Felicity Gro. L46 —4D 8
Fell St. L44 —3A 12
Felthorpe Clo. L49 —6H 9
Felton Clo. L46 —4C 8
Feltree Ho. L43 —6A 10
Fender Ct. L49 —6B 18
Fender La. L46 —4G 9
Fenderside Rd. L43 —5H 9
Fender View Rd. L46 —5G 9
Fender Way. L43 —6H 9
(in two parts)
Fenderway. L61 —5C 24
Fenwick Rd. L66 —5E 47
Fenwick St. L2 —4E 13
Ferguson Av. L49 —4D 16
Ferguson Av. L66 —1E 47
Fernbank La. L49 —6F 9
Ferndale Av. L44 —1G 11
Ferndale Av. L48 —6B 16
Ferndale Rd. L47 —5D 6
Fern Gro. L43 —2B 18
Fern Hill. L45 —3F 3
Fernhill Clo. L20 —1G 5
Fernhill Dri. L8 —1H 21
Fernhill Gdns. L20 —1G 5
Fernhill M. E. L20 —1G 5
Fernhill M. W. L20 —1G 5
Fernhill Rd. L20 —1G 5
Fernhill Way. L20 —1G 5
Fernie Cres. L8 —2H 21
Fernlea M. L43 —5A 10
Fernlea Rd. L60 —3C 30
Fernleigh. L43 —4F 19
Fern Rd. L65 —5G 47
Ferns Clo. L60 —2G 29
Ferns Rd. L63 —4D 26
Ferny Brow Rd. L49 —4H 17
Fernyess La. L64 —6A 38
Ferries Clo. L42 —1H 27
Ferry Rd. L62 —6E 35
Ferryside. L44 —3A 12
Ferry View Rd. L44 —3A 12
Festival Rd. L65 —2F 47
Ffrancon Dri. L63 —2F 27
Field Clo. L62 —1H 27
Field Hey La. L64 —4D 38
Field Rd. L45 —4F 3
Fieldside Rd. L42 —5A 20
Field St. L3 —2G 13
Fieldway. L45 —6E 3
Fieldway. L47 —6H 7
Field Way. L60 —2E 31
Fieldway. L63 —1D 26
Fieldway. L66 —6B 40
Fieldway Ct. L41 —5G 11
Fifth Av. L43 —6H 9
Finch Ct. L41 —6H 11
Finchdean Clo. L49 —3C 16
Finch Pl. L3 —3H 13
Findley Dri. L46 —2F 9
Finney, The. L48 —3B 22
Finstall Rd. L63 —1F 33
Firbrook Ct. L43 —4A 10
Firdene Cres. L43 —3C 18
Firs Av. L63 —6F 27
Firshaw Rd. L47 —4E 7
First Av. L43 —1A 18
Firs, The. L43 —5C 10
Firtree Gro. L66 —6B 46
Fir Way. L60 —6D 30
Fishers La. L61 —5A 24
Fisher St. L8 —1F 21
Fishguard Clo. L6 —1H 13
Fitzclarence Wlk. L6 —1H 13
Fitzclarence Way. L6 —1H 13
Fitzpatrick Ct. L3 —1E 13
Fitzroy Way. L6 —2H 13
Flag La. L64 —6D 36
Flail Clo. L49 —3D 16
Flambards. L49 —4H 17
Flashes La. L64 —2F 43
Flatt La. L43 —4D 18
Flatt La. L65 —1H 47
Flaxhill. L46 —4D 8
Flaybrick Clo. L43 —5C 10
Fleck La. L48 —6F 15
Fleet Croft Rd. L49 —5G 17
Fleet St. L1 —4F 13
Fleet St. L65 —2G 47
Fleming Ct. L3 —1E 13
Fleming St. L65 —1A 48
Fletcher Av. L42 —5A 20
Flint Clo. L64 —6B 36
Flint Ct. L65 —5B 48
Flint Dri. L64 —6C 36
Flint Meadow. L64 —6C 36
Flint St. L1 —6F 13
Floral Wood. L17 —5H 21
Florence Av. L60 —2B 30
Florence Rd. L44 —2A 12
Florence St. L4 —3H 5
Florence St. L41 —1H 19
Flowermead Clo. L47 —4H 7
Folds, The. L63 —5A 32
Foley Clo. L4 —4G 5
Foley St. L4 —4G 5
(in two parts)
Folly La. L44 —6C 2
Fontenoy St. L3 —2F 13
Fonthill Clo. L4 —4F 5
Fonthill Rd. L4 —3F 5
Ford Clo. L49 —3H 17
Ford Dri. L49 —2H 17
Fordham St. L4 —3G 5
Ford Hill View. L46 —5G 9
Ford La. L49 —2H 17
Ford Rd. L49 —2G 17
Fords Bldgs. L3 —2E 13
Ford St. L3 —2E 13
Ford Way. L49 —3G 17
Fordway M. L49 —3G 17
Forest Clo. L47 —4F 7
Forest Ct. L43 —1E 19
Forest Rd. L43 —6D 10
Forest Rd. L47 —4F 7
Forest Rd. L60 —2C 30
Forest Rd. L66 —6E 41
Forge Rd. L66 —1C 46
Forge St. L20 —3E 5
Fornals Grn. La. L47 —6G 7
Forrest St. L1 —5F 13
Forth St. L20 —2D 4
Fort St. L45 —4G 3
Forwood Rd. L62 —3B 34
Foster St. L20 —4E 5
Fotheringay Ct. L65 —5B 48
Fountain Rd. L45 —4F 3
Fountains Clo. L4 —4H 5
Fountains Ct. L4 —4F 5
Fountains Rd. L4 —4F 5
Fountain St. L42 —4G 19
Four Bridges. L41 —5A 12
Fourth Av. L43 —6H 9
Fowell Rd. L45 —3F 3
Foxall Way. L66 —5C 46
Foxcover Rd. L60 —4E 31
Foxcovers Rd. L63 —6G 27
Foxdale Clo. L43 —2E 19
Foxes, The. L61 —3C 24
Foxfield Rd. L47 —5F 7
Foxglove Rd. L41 —6D 10
Foxglove Way. L64 —2C 42
Fox Hey Rd. L44 —2D 10
Foxhill Clo. L8 —2H 21
Foxleigh Grange. L41 —4D 10
Fox St. L3 —1G 13
Fox St. L41 —1G 19
Foxton Clo. L46 —4B 8
Foxwood Clo. L48 —4G 15
Franceys St. L3 —4G 13
Francis Av. L43 —1F 19
Francis Av. L46 —5D 8
Frankby Av. L44 —1E 11
Frankby Clo. L49 —4B 16
Frankby Grn. L48 —5B 16
Frankby Gro. L49 —2F 17
Frankby Rd. L47 —5F 7
Frankby Rd. L48 & L49 —4F 15
Franklin Rd. L46 —1G 9
Frank St. L8 —2G 21
Fraser Pl. L3 —3G 13
Fraser St. L3 —3G 13
Freedom Clo. L7 —5H 13
Freeland St. L4 —3G 5
Freeman St. L41 —6A 12
Freemasons Row. L3 —2E 13
Frensham Clo. L63 —1F 33
Friars Clo. L63 —5F 27
Frobisher Rd. L46 —1G 9
Frobisher Rd. L64 —5C 36
Frodsham St. L4 —2H 5
Frodsham St. L41 —3A 20
Frome Clo. L61 —2H 23
Frome Ct. L65 —6H 41
Frost Dri. L61 —3G 23
Frosts M. L65 —1H 47
Fuchsia Clo. L66 —6F 47
Fuchsia Wlk. L49 —5C 16
Fulbrook Clo. L63 —1F 33
Fulbrook Rd. L63 —1F 33
Fulton Av. L48 —4G 15
Fulton St. L5 —6D 4
Fulwood Gdns. L66 —1C 46
Fulwood M. L66 —1C 46
Fulwood Rd. L66 —1C 46
Furness Clo. L49 —1E 17
Furness St. L4 —4G 5
Furrocks Clo. L64 —2D 42
Furrocks La. L64 —2D 42
Furrocks Way. L64 —2D 42
Furrows, The. L66 —6A 46
Furze Way. L46 —4E 9

Gabriel Clo. L46 —5F 9
Gainsborough Rd. L45 —6C 2
Gainsborough Rd. L49 —1F 17
Gallopers La. L61 —3D 24
Galton St. L3 —2D 12
Galtres Ct. L63 —1E 27
Galtres Pk. L63 —1E 27
Gambier Ter. L1 —6G 13
Gamlin St. L41 —5D 10
Ganney's Meadow Rd. L49 —5A 18
Garden Ct. L42 —6G 19
Garden Hey Rd. L46 —6B 8
Garden Hey Rd. L47 —4E 7
Gardenia Gro. L17 —5H 21
Garden La. L3 —1G 13
Garden La. L46 —4E 9
Gardenside. L46 —1H 9
Gardenside St. L6 —2H 13
Gardens Rd. L63 —4H 27
Gardner's Row. L3 —2F 13
Garfield Ter. L49 —2G 17
Garibaldi Ho. L5 —1G 13
Garnett Av. L4 —3F 5
Garrick Av. L46 —5C 8
Garrick Rd. L43 —1H 25
Garswood Clo. L46 —1F 9
Garswood St. L8 —4H 21
Garth Boulevd. L63 —1E 27
Gascoyne St. L3 —2E 13
Gateacre Ct. L66 —5F 41
Gautby Rd. L41 —4C 10
Gawsworth Clo. L43 —4D 18
Gawsworth Rd. L66 —2E 47
Gaypine Clo. L43 —5A 10
Gayton Av. L45 —3F 3
Gayton Av. L63 —1C 26
Gayton Farm Rd. L60 —6C 30
Gayton La. L60 —5D 30
Gayton Mill Clo. L60 —4D 30
Gayton Parkway. L60 —6E 31
Gayton Rd. L60 —4B 30
Gaytree Ct. L43 —6A 10
Gaywood Clo. L43 —6A 10
Geneva Rd. L44 —3H 11
George Rd. L47 —1E 15
Georges Dock Ga. L3 —3D 12
Georges Dockway. L3 —4D 12
Georges Pierhead. L3 —4D 12
George St. L3 —3E 13
George St. L41 —6A 12
George St. L65 —2G 41
Georgia Av. L62 —6C 28
Geraint St. L8 —1H 21
Gerald Rd. L43 —3E 19
Gerard Av. L45 —4E 3
Gerard Rd. L45 —5D 2
Gerard Rd. L48 —4D 14
Gerard St. L3 —2F 13
Gerrard Av. L66 —3C 46
Gertrude St. L41 —1B 20
Gibbs Ct. L61 —3B 24
Gibraltar Row. L3 —3D 12
Gibson Clo. L61 —6B 24
Gibson St. L8 —1H 21
Gilbert Clo. L63 —1F 33
Gilbert St. L1 —5F 13
Gildarts Gdns. L3 —1E 13
Gildart St. L3 —3G 13
Gillbrook Sq. L41 —5D 10
(off Vaughan St.)
Gills La. L61 —5C 24
Gill St. L3 —3G 13
Gilman St. L4 —4H 5
Gilmour Mt. L43 —3F 19
Gilroy Rd. L48 —4E 15
Gilwell Av. L46 —6E 9
Gilwell Clo. L46 —6E 9
Ginnel, The. L62 —4H 27
Girton Av. L20 —1G 5
Girton Clo. L65 —3B 48
Girton Rd. L65 —3B 48
Girtrell Clo. L49 —2D 16
Girtrell Rd. L49 —2D 16
Girvan Dri. L64 —1D 42
Glade, The. L47 —4F 7
Gladstone Clo. L41 —1H 19
Gladstone Hall Rd. L62 —4H 27
Gladstone Rd. L44 —2H 11
Gladstone Rd. L64 —5C 36
Gladstone St. L3 —2E 13
Gladstone St. L41 —1G 19
Gladstone Ter. L64 —5B 38
(off Neston Rd.)
Glaisher St. L5 —5H 5
Glasgow St. L42 —5B 20
Glasier Rd. L46 —4C 8
Gleaston Clo. L62 —2A 34
Gleave Sq. L6 —2H 13
Glebe Hey Rd. L49 —4G 17
Glebelands Rd. L46 —5E 9
Glebe Rd. L45 —5E 3
Glebeway Rd. L65 —2D 48
Gleggside. L48 —5E 15
Glegg St. L3 —1D 12
Glenalmond Rd. L44 —1H 11
Glenathol Rd. L66 —3C 46
Glenavon Rd. L43 —6E 19
Glenburn Av. L62 —1G 39
Glenburn Rd. L44 —2H 11
Glencoe Rd. L45 —5F 3
Glencoe Rd. L66 —3C 46
Glendale Clo. L8 —4H 21
Glendale Gro. L63 —1H 33
Glendower St. L20 —2E 5
Glendyke Rd. L66 —3C 46
Gleneagles Clo. L61 —6B 24
Gleneagles Rd. L66 —2C 46
Glenesk Rd. L66 —3C 46
Glenfield Clo. L43 —5A 10
Glenfield Clo. L46 —4B 8
Glenmarsh Clo. L63 —4D 26
Glenmaye Rd. L66 —3C 46
Glenmore Rd. L43 —3E 19
Glen Pk. Rd. L45 —4E 3
Glen Rd. L66 —2C 46
Glen Ronald Dri. L49 —2D 16
Glen, The. L62 —6A 28
Glen, The. L63 —6A 28
Glenton Pk. L64 —1D 42
Glentree Clo. L49 —2D 16
Glenvale Wlk. L6 —1H 13
Glenwood Clo. L66 —1C 46
Glenwood Dri. L61 —2A 24
Glenwood Gdns. L66 —1C 46
Glenwood Rd. L66 —1C 46
Globe St. L4 —4G 5
Gloucester Clo. L66 —6A 46
Gloucester Pl. L6 —2H 13
Gloucester Rd. L45 —5C 2
Gloucester St. L3 —3F 13
Glover St. L8 —1F 21
Glover St. L42 —3G 19
Glyn Av. L62 —4C 34
Glyn Rd. L44 —6F 3
Golden Gro. L4 —2H 5
Goldie St. L4 —4H 5
Goldsmith Rd. L43 —6D 18
Goldsmith Way. L43 —6D 18
Golf Links Rd. L42 —6F 19
Gonville Rd. L20 —1F 5
Goodakers Ct. L49 —5G 17
(off Fleet Croft Rd.)
Goodakers Meadow. L49 —5G 17
Goodall Pl. L4 —2G 5
Goodall St. L4 —2G 5
Goodison Av. L4 —3H 5
Goodison Pl. L4 —2H 5
Goodison Rd. L4 —2H 5
Goodwin Av. L41 —4B 10
Goodwood Gro. L66 —4D 46
Goodwood St. L5 —6F 5
Goose Grn., The. L47 —4F 7
Goostrey Clo. L63 —2H 33
Gordon Av. L49 —4E 17

Gordon Av. L62 —4C 34
Gordon Ct. L49 —4E 17
Gordon Rd. L45 —4G 3
Gordon St. L41 —1G 19
Gordon Ter. L64 —5B 38
(off Neston Rd.)
Goree. L2 —4D 12
Gore St. L8 —1G 21
Gorsebank St. L44 —2G 11
Gorse Cres. L44 —3G 11
Gorsedale Pk. L44 —3H 11
Gorsedale Rd. L44 —3F 11
Gorsefield Av. L62 —6B 34
Gorsefield Clo. L62 —6B 34
Gorsefield Rd. L42 —4G 19
Gorsehill Rd. L45 —4E 3
Gorsehill Rd. L60 —2C 30
Gorse La. L48 —6G 15
Gorse Rd. L47 —5F 7
Gorseyville Cres. L63 —4E 27
Gorseyville Rd. L63 —4E 27
Gorstons La. L64 —1E 43
Gorst St. L4 —4H 5
Gowy Ct. L66 —5E 41
Grace Rd. L65 —1H 47
Grace St. L8 —3H 21
Gradwell St. L1 —4F 13
Grafton Cres. L8 —1G 21
Grafton Dri. L49 —3G 17
Grafton Gro. L8 —3G 21
Grafton Rd. L45 —4F 3
Grafton Rd. L65 —2G 41
Grafton St. L8 —1F 21
Grafton St. L43 —2F 19
Grafton Wlk. L48 —5E 15
Graham Av. L66 —2D 46
Graham Rd. L48 —4C 14
Grainger Av. L43 —5D 18
Grainger Av. L48 —5D 14
Grain Ind. Est. L8 —3G 21
Grain St. L8 —3H 21
Grammar School La. L48
  —6F 15
Grampian Av. L46 —5E 9
Grampian Way. L46 —5E 9
Grampian Way. L62 —6C 34
Grampian Way. L64 —2C 42
Granby Cres. L63 —1G 33
Grange Av. L45 —5F 3
Grange Cres. L66 —4A 40
Grange Cross Clo. L48 —6G 15
Grange Cross La. L48 —6G 15
Grange Dri. L60 —2B 30
Grange Dri. L63 —4A 32
Grange Farm Cres. L48 —4G 15
Grange Mt. L43 —2G 19
Grange Mt. L48 —5F 15
Grange Mt. L60 —2B 30
Grange Old Rd. L48 —5E 15
Grange Pavement. L41 —1A 20
Grange Pl. L41 —1G 19
Grange Rd. L41 —1H 19
Grange Rd. L48 —5D 14
Grange Rd. L60 —1B 30
Grange Rd. E. L41 —1A 20
Grange Rd. W. L43 & L41
  —1F 19
Grange, The. L44 —1G 11
Grange Vale. L42 —6C 20
Grantham Clo. L54 —6A 24
Granton Rd. L5 —5H 5
Grant Rd. L14 —1F 25
Granville Clo. L45 —5C 2
Granville Dri. L66 —6B 40
Grappenhall Rd. L65 —3F 47
Grasmere Av. L43 —2A 18
Grasmere Dri. L45 —6E 3

Grasmere Rd. L64 —1C 42
Grasmere Rd. L65 —5A 48
Grassmoor Clo. L62 —3C 34
Grassville Rd. L42 —4A 20
Grass Wood Rd. L49 —5H 17
Gratrix Rd. L62 —3B 34
Graylands Rd. L62 —3A 28
Grayson St. L1 —5E 13
Greasby Dri. L66 —3E 47
Greasby Hill Rd. L48 —6E 15
Greasby Rd. L44 —1E 11
Greasby Rd. L49 —4C 16
Gt. Charlotte St. L1 —3F 13
Gt. Crosshall St. L3 —3E 13
Gt. George Pl. L1 —6G 13
Gt. George Sq. L1 —6G 13
Gt. George St. L1 —6G 13
Gt. Homer St. L5 —5E 5
Gt. Howard St. L3 & L5 —2D 12
Gt. Mersey St. L5 —5F 5
(in two parts)
Gt. Nelson St. L3 —1F 13
Gt. Newton St. L3 —3H 13
Gt. Orford St. L3 —4H 13
Gt. Richmond St. L3 —2F 13
Gt. Western Ho. L41 —6B 12
Greaves St. L8 —2H 21
Grecian Ter. L5 —5G 5
Greek St. L3 —3G 13
Greenacre Dri. L63 —4A 34
Greenacres Clo. L43 —5A 10
Greenacres Ct. L43 —5A 10
Green Acres Est. L49 —5C 16
Green Bank. L63 —1A 32
Greenbank Av. L45 —4F 3
Greenbank Av. L66 —6C 40
Greenbank Dri. L61 —6C 24
Greenbank Rd. L42 —3G 19
Greenbank Rd. L48 —3D 14
Greencroft Rd. L44 —2G 11
Greendale Rd. L62 —3G 27
Greenfield La. L60 —1G 29
Greenfield Rd. L66 —6B 40
Greenfields Av. L62 —4A 34
Greenfields Clo. L64 —2D 42
Greenfields Cres. L62 —4A 34
Greenfields Croft. L64 —2C 42
Greenfields Dri. L64 —2C 42
Greenfield Way. L44 —1F 11
Greengates Cres. L64 —2C 42
Green Haven. L43 —2B 18
Greenheath Way. L46 —2F 9
Greenhey Clo. L43 —2G 25
Greenheys Rd. L44 —2F 11
Greenheys Rd. L61 —4G 23
Greenhow Av. L48 —4D 14
Greenland St. L1 —6F 13
Green La. L3 —4G 13
Green La. L41 —3A 20
Green La. L45 —6A 2
(in two parts)
Green La. L62 —3C 34
Green La. L63 —4F 27
Green La. L65 —3A 48
Green La. L66 —3C 46
(in four parts)
Green Lawn. L42 —6B 20
Green Lawn Gro. L42 —6B 20
Green Lawns Dri. L66 —6A 46
Greenlea Clo. L63 —3F 27
Greenlea Clo. L65 —5H 47
Greenleas Rd. L45 —5B 2
Green Mt. L49 —2G 17
Greenock St. L3 —2D 12
Greenside. L6 —2H 13
Green St. L5 —1E 13
Green, The. L48 —2B 22
Green, The. L62 —4C 28
Green, The. L64 —1D 42
(Nessholt)
Green, The. L64 —5B 36
(Neston)
Green, The. L64 —5B 38
(Willaston)
Green, The. L65 —5H 47

Greenville Clo. L63 —4F 27
Greenville Rd. L63 —4F 27
Green Way. L61 —5A 24
Greenway. L62 —6B 28
Greenway. L49 —3E 17
Greenway Rd. L42 —4H 19
Greenwood Clo. L44 —6G 3
Greenwood Rd. L47 —4G 7
Greenwood Rd. L49 —4G 17
Greetham St. L1 —5F 13
Gregson Ct. L45 —3G 3
Gregson St. L6 —2H 13
Gregson Way. L6 —2H 13
Greig Way. L8 —3H 21
Grenfell Clo. L64 —4A 36
Grenfell Rd. L64 —4A 36
Grenville Cres. L63 —4A 34
Grenville Dri. L61 —6A 24
Grenville Rd. L42 —4B 20
Grenville Rd. L64 —4C 36
Grenville St. S. L1 —5F 13
Grenville Way. L42 —4B 20
Gresford Av. L43 —5E 19
Gresford Av. L48 —4E 15
Gresford Pl. L44 —1H 11
Greta St. L8 —2H 21
Greystoke Clo. L49 —3F 17
Greystones. L66 —3D 46
Griffin Av. L46 —5E 9
Griffiths Clo. L49 —4C 16
Griffiths St. L1 —5G 13
Grimshaw St. L20 —1D 4
Grindley Gdns. L65 —5A 48
Grinshill Clo. L8 —1H 21
Grisedale Rd. L62 —3C 34
Grizedale Rd. L5 —6H 5
Grosvenor Av. L48 —5D 14
Grosvenor Ct. L43 —2F 19
Grosvenor Dri. L45 —3F 3
Grosvenor Pl. L43 —2E 19
Grosvenor Rd. L4 —1G 5
Grosvenor Rd. L43 —1E 19
Grosvenor Rd. L45 —3F 3
Grosvenor Rd. L47 —1D 14
Grosvenor St. L3 —1F 13
Grosvenor St. L44 —6F 3
Grove Av. L60 —2B 30
Grove Clo. L8 —6H 13
Groveland Av. L45 —5B 2
Groveland Av. L47 —6D 6
Groveland Rd. L45 —4B 2
Grove Pk. L8 —6H 13
Grove Pl. L4 —4G 5
Grove Pl. L47 —6D 6
Grove Rd. L42 —5B 20
Grove Rd. L45 —5C 2
Grove Rd. L47 —6D 6
Grove Side. L7 —5H 13
Groveside. L48 —5C 14
Grove Sq. L62 —2G 27
Groves, The. L8 —6H 13
Groves, The. L43 —2E 19
Groves, The. L66 —6B 46
Grove St. L7 —5H 13
Grove St. L62 —2H 27
Grove Ter. L47 —6D 6
Grove, The. L44 —3H 11
Grove, The. L44 —3G 11
Grove Way. L7 —5H 13
Grovewood Ct. L43 —4G 19
Grundy St. L5 —5D 4
Guardian Ct. L48 —6E 15
Guelph Pl. L7 —3H 13
Guelph St. L7 —3H 13
Guernsey Dri. L65 —5A 48
Guffitt's Clo. L47 —4G 7
Guffitt's Rake. L47 —4G 7
Guildford Clo. L6 —2H 13
Guildford St. L44 —1H 11
Gulls Way. L60 —3H 29
Gunn Gro. L64 —5D 36
Gurnall St. L4 —4H 5
Gwendoline Clo. L61 —4C 24

Gwendoline St. L8 —1H 21
Gwent St. L8 —1H 21
Gwladys St. L4 —2H 5
Gwydir St. L8 —2H 21

H

Hackins Hey. L2 —3E 13
Hackthorpe St. L4 —4G 5
Haddock St. L20 —2D 4
Haddon Dri. L61 —5B 24
Haddon St. L64 —3F 43
(in two parts)
Haddon Rd. L42 —5C 20
Hadfield Av. L47 —6E 7
Hadley Av. L62 —3A 34
Hadlow Gdns. L42 —3H 19
Hadlow La. L64 —5B 38
Hadlow Rd. L64 —2B 44
Hadlow Ter. L64 —6B 38
Hadwens Bldgs. L3 —3E 13
Hahneman Rd. L4 —1G 5
Haig Av. L46 —5F 9
Haigh St. L3 —1H 13
(in two parts)
Halcyon Rd. L41 —3G 19
Haldane Av. L41 —6D 10
Haldane Rd. L4 —1H 5
Hale Rd. L4 —2G 5
Hale Rd. L45 —6G 3
Hale St. L2 —3E 13
Halkyn Dri. L5 —6H 5
Hall Dri. L49 —4C 16
Hallfield Pk. L66 —3D 46
Hall La. L7 —3H 13
Hallville Rd. L44 —2G 11
Hallwood Clo. L64 —6C 36
Halsall Grn. L63 —2H 33
Halsbury Rd. L45 —5F 3
Halstead Rd. L44 —2G 11
Halton Cres. L49 —4B 16
Halton Cres. L66 —5F 47
Halton Rd. L45 —5E 3
Halton Rd. L66 —6E 47
Halton Way. L66 —6E 47
Hambledon Dri. L49 —3C 16
Hambleton Clo. L66 —1A 46
Hamil Clo. L47 —4G 7
Hamilton Clo. L64 —3A 36
Hamilton Ct. L60 —5D 30
Hamilton La. L41 —6A 12
Hamilton Rd. L5 —6H 5
Hamilton Rd. L45 —3F 3
Hamilton Sq. L41 —6A 12
Hamilton St. L41 —1B 20
Hamlet Rd. L45 —5D 2
Hampden Gro. L42 —3H 19
Hampden Rd. L42 —3H 19
Hampden St. L4 —1H 5
Hampstead Rd. L44 —2G 11
Hampton Clo. L64 —1C 42
Hampton Gdns. L65 —2G 47
Hampton St. L8 —6H 13
Handfield Pl. L5 —6H 5
Handfield St. L5 —6H 5
Handford Av. L62 —6D 34
Hankin St. L5 —4D 4
Hanley Clo. L61 —6A 24
Hanns Hall Rd. L64 —5G 37
Hanover Clo. L43 —1D 18
Hanover St. L1 —5E 13
Hanson Pk. L43 —2C 18
Hapton St. L5 —5G 5
Harborne Rd. L63 —1F 33
Harcourt Av. L44 —2A 12
Harcourt St. L4 —4G 5
Harcourt St. L41 —6G 11
Hardie Av. L46 —4C 8
Harding Av. L41 —4B 10
Harding Av. L63 —5F 27
Harding Clo. L5 —6H 5
Hardknott Rd. L62 —2C 34
Hardman St. L1 —5G 13
Hardy Clo. L66 —4E 47
Hardy St. L1 —5G 13
(in two parts)

Harebell St. L5 —4F 5
Harewood Av. L66 —3B 46
Harewood Rd. L45 —4E 3
Harfield Gdns. L66 —2C 46
Hargrave Av. L43 —4C 18
Hargrave Clo. L43 —4C 18
Hargrave Dri. L66 —2E 47
Hargrave La. L63 —6F 33
Harker St. L3 —2G 13
Harland Rd. L42 —3H 19
Harlech Clo. L63 —5F 27
Harlech Ct. L65 —4B 48
Harlech St. L4 —2G 5
Harlech St. L44 —4A 12
Harlech Way. L65 —4B 48
Harley Av. L63 —1C 26
Harlian Av. L46 —6D 8
Harlow St. L8 —3G 21
Harn, The. L64 —4C 46
Harper Clo. L66 —3D 46
Harper St. L6 —3H 13
Harrington Av. L47 —6E 7
Harrington Rd. L3 —3G 21
Harrington St. L2 —4E 13
Harrington View. L44 —6H 3
Harris Clo. L63 —1G 33
Harrison Dri. L45 —3B 2
Harrisons Ter. L66 —1C 46
Harrison's Yd. L62 —6D 34
Harrison Way. L3 —3G 21
Harrock Wood Clo. L61 —3A 24
Harrogate Clo. L62 —1F 39
Harrogate Dri. L5 —6H 5
Harrogate Rd. L42 —1G 27
Harrogate Rd. L62 —1F 39
Harrogate Wlk. L42 —1G 27
Harrowby Rd. L42 —3H 19
Harrowby Rd. L44 —1A 12
Harrowby Rd. S. L42 —3G 19
Harrowby St. L8 —6H 13
Harrow Clo. L4 —6D 2
Harrow Gro. L62 —3B 34
Harrow Rd. L4 —6D 2
Harrow Rd. L65 —3B 48
Hartford Clo. L43 —4D 18
Hartford Dri. L65 —3F 47
Harthill M. L43 —4A 10
Hartington Av. L41 —6F 11
Hartington Rd. L4 —2H 11
Hartismere Rd. L44 —2H 11
Hartley Clo. L4 —4H 5
Hartley Quay. L3 —5E 13
Hartnup St. L5 —5H 5
(in two parts)
Hart St. L3 —3G 13
Harvester Way. L49 —3C 16
Harvest La. L46 —4D 8
Harvey Av. L49 —4D 16
Harvey Rd. L45 —5E 3
Hassal Rd. L62 —1G 27
Hatchmere Clo. L43 —4D 18
Hatherley St. L8 —6H 13
Hatherley St. L44 —3A 12
Hatton Av. L62 —2G 39
Hatton Clo. L60 —2B 30
Hatton Garden. L3 —3E 13
Hawarden Av. L43 —1G 19
Hawarden Av. L44 —1G 11
Hawarden Ct. L63 —5F 27
Hawarden Gdns. L65 —5B 48
Hawick Clo. L64 —2H 45
Hawke Grn. L64 —2H 45
Hawke St. L3 —3G 13
Hawkins Rd. L64 —4C 36
Hawksmore Clo. L49 —1D 16
Hawks Way. L60 —3A 30
Hawthorn Dri. L48 —5G 15
Hawthorn Dri. L61 —6B 24
Hawthorne Dri. L64 —4D 38
Hawthorne Gro. L44 —3A 12
Hawthorne Rd. L20 —1H 5
Hawthorne Rd. L44 —1H 11
Hawthorn La. L62 —3B 34
Hawthorn Rd. L44 —1H 11
Hawthorn Rd. L66 —1C 46
Haycroft Clo. L66 —5D 46
Haydock Rd. L45 —4G 3
Hayfield Pl. L46 —5G 9

Hayfield St. L4 —4H 5
Haylock Clo. L8 —3H 21
Hazel Ct. L8 —3H 21
(off Byles St.)
Hazeldene Av. L45 —6E 3
Hazeldene Av. L61 —3D 24
Hazeldene Way. L61 —3D 24
Hazel Gro. L61 —2H 23
Hazel Gro. L63 —5E 27
Hazel Rd. L41 —2H 19
Hazel Rd. L47 —5E 7
Hazelwood. L49 —2D 16
Headington Rd. L49 —2D 16
Headland Clo. L48 —6D 14
Head St. L8 —1G 21
Heath Av. L65 —6G 47
Heathbank Av. L46 —2E 11
Heathbank Av. L61 —2G 23
Heathbank Rd. L42 —4H 19
Heath Clo. L48 —4C 22
Heathcote Gdns. L63 —4F 27
Heathcote Rd. L4 —1H 5
Heath Dale. L63 —6F 27
Heath Dri. L49 —2G 17
Heath Dri. L60 —2B 30
Heather Bank. L63 —3D 26
Heather Brow. L43 —1D 18
Heather Clo. L4 —4H 5
Heather Clo. L66 —4E 47
Heather Ct. L4 —3H 5
Heatherdale. L41 —4G 19
Heatherdale Clo. L42 —4G 19
Heather Dene. L62 —6B 28
Heatheredge Rd. L48 —4D 14
Heatherland. L49 —3H 17
Heather Rd. L60 —2C 30
Heather Rd. L63 —5D 26
Heathfield. L62 —1B 34
Heathfield Rd. L41 —3G 19
Heathfield Rd. L63 —4F 27
Heathfield Rd. L65 —2H 47
Heathfield St. L1 —4G 13
Heath Gro. L66 —6B 40
Heathlands. L66 —1B 46
Heathlands, The. L46 —1E 9
Heath La. L64 & L66 —4E 39
Heath Moor Rd. L46 —4D 8
Heath Rd. L43 —4E 27
Heathside. L60 —2H 29
Heathway. L60 —4D 30
Hector Pl. L20 —2F 5
Helena St. L9 —1H 5
Helena St. L41 —2D 20
Helmingham Gro. L41 —3A 20
Helmingham Rd. L41 —3A 20
Helsby Av. L62 —2H 39
Helton Clo. L43 —4C 18
Hemingford St. L41 —1H 19
Hemsworth Av. L66 —2C 46
Henderson Clo. L49 —1D 16
Hendon Wlk. L49 —4C 16
Henglers Clo. L6 —2H 13
Henley Clo. L63 —1G 33
Henley Clo. L64 —1C 42
Henley Rd. L64 —1C 42
Henry Edward St. L3 —2E 13
Henry St. L1 —5F 13
Henry St. L41 —1A 20
Henthorne Rd. L62 —1H 27
Henthorne St. L43 —2G 19
Herbert Pl. L41 —1A 20
Herberts La. L60 —4B 30
Herculaneum Ct. L8 —4H 21
Herculaneum Rd. L8 —3G 21
Hereford Av. L49 —1F 17
Hereford Av. L66 —4A 46
Heriot St. L5 —5F 5
Heriot Wlk. L5 —5F 5
Heron Ct. L64 —4A 36
Heronpark Way. L63 —1H 33
Heron Rd. L47 —6H 7
Heron Rd. L20 —1F 5
Herschell St. L5 —5H 5
Hertford Dri. L65 —5G 3
Hertford Rd. L20 —1E 5
Hesketh Av. L42 —6H 19

Hesketh Dri. L60 —2C 30
Hessle Dri. L60 —4B 30
Hesslewell Ct. L60 —2C 30
Heswall Av. L63 —1C 26
Heswall Mt. L61 —4C 24
Heswall Rd. L66 —3D 46
Hewitts Pl. L2 —3E 13
Heyes Dri. L45 —1A 10
Heyes St. L5 —6H 5
Heyfield Pk. Rd. L66 —6B 40
Heygarth Dri. L49 —3D 16
Heygarth Rd. L62 —6C 34
Heys Av. L62 —3B 34
Heythrop Dri. L60 —3F 31
Heyville Rd. L63 —3E 27
Heywood Boulevd. L61 —3C 24
Heywood Clo. L61 —3C 24
Heywood Rd. L66 —2C 46
Heyworth St. L5 —6H 5
Hickmans Rd. L41 —4F 11
Highacre Rd. L45 —4E 3
Higham Sq. L5 —1G 13
High Bank Clo. L43 —2B 18
Highcroft Av. L63 —4G 27
Highcroft, The. L63 —4F 27
Higher Bebington Rd. L63 —3E 27
Highfield Clo. L44 —1E 11
Highfield Clo. L64 —5C 36
Highfield Cres. L42 —6B 20
Highfield Dri. L49 —3D 16
Highfield Gro. L42 —6B 20
Highfield Rd. L42 —5B 20
Highfield Rd. L64 —5C 36
Highfield Rd. L65 —2A 48
Highfield Rd. L66 —1B 46
Highfield Rd. N. L65 —1A 48
Highfields. L60 —2B 30
Highfield S. L42 —2F 27
Highfield St. L3 —2E 13
(in two parts)
Highgate Clo. L60 —1B 30
Highgreen Rd. L42 —4G 19
Highpark Rd. L42 —4G 19
High Pk. St. L8 —2H 21
High St. Bromborough, L62 —2C 34
High St. Neston, L64 —5C 36
Hilary Dri. L49 —1G 17
Hilbre Av. L44 —1E 11
Hilbre Av. L60 —5A 30
Hilbre Ct. L48 —6C 14
Hilbre Rd. L48 —6D 14
Hilbre St. L3 —4G 13
Hilbre St. L41 —5H 11
Hilbre View. L48 —5E 15
Hillam Rd. L45 —5B 2
Hillary Rd. L62 —6B 34
Hill Bark Rd. L48 —5B 16
Hill Clo. L64 —2F 43
Hill Ct. L64 —2F 43
Hill Crest. L20 —1G 5
Hillcrest Dri. L49 —4C 16
Hillcrest Dri. L66 —1A 46
Hillcrest Rd. L66 —1B 46
Hillcroft Rd. L44 —2G 11
Hillfield Dri. L61 —1B 30
Hillfield Rd. L66 —6D 40
Hillfoot Clo. L43 —5A 10
Hill Gro. L46 —6E 9
Hillhead Rd. L20 —1G 5
Hillingdon Av. L61 —1B 30
Hill Ridge. L43 —2B 18
Hill Rd. L43 —6C 10
Hillsdown Way. L66 —5C 46
Hillside Clo. L20 —1G 5
Hillside Ct. L41 —3A 20
Hillside Dri. L66 —5E 41
Hillside Rd. L41 —3A 20
Hillside Rd. L43 —5B 10
Hillside Rd. L44 —1C 10
Hillside Rd. L48 —5F 15
Hillside Rd. L60 —4C 30
Hillside St. L6 —2H 13
Hillside View. L43 —4E 19
Hill St. L8 —1F 21
(in two parts)
Hill St. Bus. Cen. L8 —1F 21
(off Hill St.)
Hilltop La. L60 —3D 30
Hill Top La. L64 —2F 43
Hillview Av. L48 —4D 14
Hillview Ct. L43 —5A 10
Hill View Dri. L49 —1G 17
Hillview Mans. L48 —4D 14
(off Lang La.)
Hill View Rd. L61 —2G 23
Hillwood Clo. L63 —2F 33
Hilton Clo. L41 —1H 19
Hilton Gro. L48 —4C 14
Hinderton Dri. L48 —6G 15
Hinderton Dri. L60 —5B 30
Hinderton La. L64 —4E 37
Hinderton Rd. L41 —2A 20
Hinderton Rd. L64 —5D 36
Hind St. L41 —2A 20
Hinson St. L41 —1A 20
Hobart St. L5 —5G 5
Hobhouse Ct. L43 —1F 19
Hoblyn Rd. L43 —5C 10
Hockenhall All. L2 —3E 13
Hockenhull Clo. L63 —1G 33
Hodder Pl. L5 —5H 5
Hodder St. L5 —5G 5
Hodson Pl. L6 —1H 13
Hogarth Wlk. L4 —3F 5
Holborn Hill. L41 —3A 20
Holborn Sq. L41 —3A 20
Holborn St. L6 —3H 13
Holcombe Clo. L49 —3D 16
Holin Ct. L43 —6D 10
Holland Gro. L60 —2B 30
Holland Rd. L45 —4G 3
Hollows, The. L48 —3B 22
Holly Av. L63 —6F 27
Hollybank Rd. L41 —2H 19
Holly Ct. L5 —5H 5
Hollyfield Rd. L65 —2H 47
Holly Gro. L42 —3A 20
Holly Pl. L46 —6F 9
Holly Rd. L65 —2A 48
Holm Cotts. L43 —5D 18
Holmcrofts. L64 —2C 42
Holme St. L5 —4D 4
Holmesway. L61 —5B 24
Holmfield. L43 —5D 18
Holmfield Dri. L66 —4D 46
Holm Hey Rd. L43 —6D 18
Holmlands Cres. L43 —5C 18
Holmlands Dri. L43 —4C 18
Holmlands Way. L43 —5D 18
Holm La. L43 —5D 18
Holm Oak Way. L66 —6A 46
Holmside Clo. L46 —5F 9
Holmside La. L43 —5D 18
Holm View Clo. L43 —4E 19
Holmville Rd. L63 —4E 27
Holmway. L63 —4F 27
Holmwood Av. L61 —4E 25
Holmwood Dri. L61 —4E 25
Holmwood Dri. L65 —4H 47
Holt Av. L46 —5E 9
Holt Hey. L64 —2E 43
Holt Hill. L41 —3A 20
Holt Hill Ter. L41 —3A 20
Holt Hill Ter. L42 —3A 20
Holt Rd. L41 —3A 20
Holy Cross Clo. L3 —2F 13
Holywell Clo. L64 —4A 36
Home Farm Clo. L49 —5A 18
Home Farm Rd. L49 —5H 17
Homestead M. L48 —4D 14
Honeysuckle Clo. L66 —6A 46
Hood St. L44 —2H 11
Hookstone Dri. L66 —1C 46
Hoole Rd. L49 —4H 17
Hoose Ct. L47 —5E 7
Hooton Grn. L66 —3A 40
Hooton La. L66 —4B 40
Hooton Rd. L64 & L66 —5C 38
Hooton Way. L66 —3H 39
Hooton Works Ind. Est. L66 —4G 39
Hope Cotts. L66 —5A 40
Hope Croft. L66 —5F 47
Hope Farm Precinct. L66 —5F 47
Hope Farm Rd. L66 —6E 47
Hope Pl. L1 —5G 13
Hope St. L1 —6G 13
Hope St. L41 —6H 11
Hope St. L45 —3F 3
Hope Ter. L42 —4H 19
Hope Way. L8 —5H 13
Hopfield Rd. L46 —5F 9
Hopwood St. L5 —6E 5
(in two parts)
Horace Black Gdns. L65 —1A 48
Horatio St. L41 —1H 19
Horbury Gdns. L66 —2C 46
Hornbeam Av. L66 —6F 47
Hornbeam Clo. L46 —5B 8
Hornby Av. L62 —2A 34
Hornby Ct. L62 —2A 34
Hornby Rd. L62 —2A 34
Hornby St. L5 —1F 13
Hornby St. L41 —1B 20
Hornby Wlk. L5 —1E 13
Horseman Pl. L44 —3A 12
Horsfall Gro. L8 —3G 21
Horsfall St. L8 —3G 21
Horstone Cres. L66 —5F 47
Horstone Gdns. L66 —5F 47
Horstone Rd. L66 —5F 47
Hoscote Pk. L48 —5C 14
Hose Side Rd. L45 —4D 2
Hospital Rd. L62 —3H 27
Hotham St. L3 —3G 13
Hothfield Rd. L44 —2H 11
Hotspur St. L20 —2E 5
Houghton Ct. L49 —4H 17
Houghton La. L1 —4F 13
Houghton Rd. L49 —3H 17
Houghton St. L1 —4F 13
Houghton Way. L1 —4F 13
(off St John's Precinct)
Hourd Way. L66 —6A 46
Howard Av. L62 —3B 34
Howard Ct. L64 —4D 36
Howards Rd. L61 —3D 24
Howards Way. L64 —1E 43
Howbeck Clo. L43 —1D 18
Howbeck Ct. L43 —2D 18
Howbeck Dri. L43 —1D 18
Howbeck Rd. L43 —2D 18
Howell Dri. L49 —5D 16
Howells Av. L66 —4C 46
Howe St. L20 —2D 4
Howson St. L42 —5B 20
Hoyer Ind. Est. L65 —3D 48
Hoylake Rd. L43 & L41 —3B 10
Hoylake Rd. L46 —6B 8
Hoyle Rd. L47 —5D 6
Huddleston Clo. L49 —4A 18
Hudson Rd. L46 —1G 9
Hughes La. L43 —4F 19
Hughson St. L8 —2G 21
Hulmewood. L63 —2G 27
Humber Clo. L4 —3G 5
Humber Rd. L66 —5F 47
Humber St. L41 —4D 10
Hume Ct. L47 —5E 7
Hummocks Dri. L48 —3B 22
Hunstanton Clo. L49 —6G 9
Hunter St. L3 —3F 13
Hunters Way. L64 —5A 36
Huntington Clo. L46 —5B 8
Hurford Av. L65 —3F 47
Hurrell Rd. L41 —4B 10
Hurst Bank. L42 —1F 27
Hurst St. L1 —5E 13
(in two parts)
Huskisson St. L8 —6H 13
Huxley Clo. L46 —5B 8
Huxley Ct. L66 —5F 41
Hyde Clo. L65 —3F 47
Hydro Av. L48 —6D 14
Hylton Av. L44 —1E 11
Hylton Ct. L65 —5C 48
Hyslop St. L8 —1G 21

Iffley Clo. L49 —2D 16
Ikin Clo. L43 —4A 10
Ilchester Rd. L41 —4D 10
Ilchester Rd. L44 —2H 11
Ilford Av. L44 —3F 11
Ilford St. L3 —3G 13
Iliad St. L5 —1G 13
Ilsley Clo. L49 —3F 17
Imison St. L9 —1G 5
Imison Way. L9 —1G 5
Imperial Av. L45 —5G 3
Imperial M. L65 —1H 47
Imrie St. L4 —1H 5
Ince Av. L62 —2G 39
Ince Clo. L43 —4D 18
Ince Gro. L43 —3D 18
Inchcape Rd. L45 —6B 2
Index St. L4 —2H 5
Ingestre Rd. L43 —4E 19
Ingleborough Rd. L42 —5H 19
Ingleby Rd. L44 —2E 11
Ingleby Rd. L62 —1H 27
Inglegreen. L60 —3D 30
Inglemere Rd. L42 —5A 20
Ingleton Clo. L49 —3D 16
Inglewood. L46 —6D 8
Inglewood Av. L46 —6D 8
Inley Clo. L63 —1G 33
Inley Rd. L63 —1F 33
Inman Rd. L49 —1E 17
Innisfree Clo. L66 —2C 46
Intake Clo. L64 —5C 38
International Bus. & Management Cen. L41 —1A 20
Inveresk Ct. L43 —1C 18
Inward Way. L65 —6H 41
Ionic St. L42 —5B 20
Irby Av. L44 —1E 11
Irby Clo. L66 —3E 47
Irby Rd. L61 —4H 23
Irbyside Rd. L48 —6B 16
Ireton St. L4 —1H 5
Iris Av. L41 —5D 10
Irvine Rd. L42 —5H 19
Irvine Ter. L62 —1A 28
Irwell St. L3 —4D 12
Isaac St. L8 —3H 21
Islington. L3 —3G 13
Islington Sq. L3 —2H 13
Islip Clo. L61 —2H 23
Ismay Dri. L44 —6H 3
Ismay St. L4 —2H 5
Ivor Rd. L44 —6G 3
Ivy Av. L63 —4E 27
Ivydale Rd. L42 —4A 20
Ivy Farm Dri. L64 —1D 42
Ivy La. L46 —3E 9
Ivy St. L41 —1B 20

Jack McBain Ct. L3 —1E 13
Jackson Clo. L63 —1F 27
Jackson Ho. L42 —5B 20
Jackson Quay. L3 —1F 21
Jackson St. L41 —2A 20
Jacob St. L8 —3H 21
Jamaica St. L1 —6F 13
James Av. L66 —4C 46
Jamesbrook Clo. L41 —5E 11
James Clarke St. L5 —1E 13
James Hopkins Way. L4 —4F 5
James Larkin Way. L4 —4F 5
James St. L2 —4E 13
James St. L41 —3G 19
James St. L43 —3G 19
James St. L44 —3A 12
Jarrow Clo. L43 —3F 19
Jasmine Clo. L5 —6H 5
Jasmine Clo. L49 —6D 8
Jasmine M. L17 —4H 21
Jason St. L5 —5G 5
Jason Wlk. L5 —5G 5
Jedborough Av. L66 —1H 45
Jeffreys Dri. L49 —2D 16
Jellicoe Clo. L48 —3B 22
Jenkinson St. L3 —2G 13
Jersey Av. L65 —6A 48
Jessamine Rd. L42 —4A 20
Jessica Ho. L20 —2F 5
Joan Av. L46 —5D 8
Joan Av. L49 —3E 17
Jocelyn Clo. L63 —6G 27
John Bagot Clo. L5 —6G 5
John F. Kennedy Heights. L3 —1G 13
John Moores Clo. L7 —5H 13
John Nicholas Cres. L65 —1A 48
Johnson Rd. L43 —6D 18
Johnson St. L3 —3E 13
John St. L3 —2G 13
John St. L41 —6B 12
John St. L65 —1H 47
John Willis Ho. L42 —5C 20
Jonson Rd. L64 —4C 36
Jordan St. L1 —6F 13
Joseph Groome Towers. L65 —1A 48
Jubilee Cres. L62 —4H 27
Jubilee Dri. L48 —3D 14
Jubilee Gro. L44 —2H 11
Juliet Av. L63 —2E 27
Juliet Gdns. L63 —2E 27
June Av. L62 —3B 34
Juniper Clo. L49 —5C 16
Juniper Dri. L66 —6E 47
Juniper Gro. L66 —6F 47
Juniper St. L20 —3E 5
Juvenal Pl. L3 —1G 13
Juvenal St. L3 —1F 13

Kale Clo. L48 —6D 14
Karen Way. L66 —4D 46
Karslake Rd. L44 —3H 11
Kearsley Clo. L4 —4G 5
Kearsley St. L4 —4G 5
Keats Clo. L66 —6A 46
Keble Dri. L45 —5B 2
Keble Rd. L20 —1E 5
Keele Clo. L43 —3A 10
Keepers La. L63 —4B 26
Keighley Av. L45 —6C 2
Keightley St. L41 —6H 11
Keir Murren Ho. L8 —2H 21
Keith Av. L4 —2H 5
Keith Dri. L63 —6A 34
Kellet's Pl. L42 —4B 20
Kellett Rd. L46 —2H 9
Kelmscott Dri. L44 —1C 10
Kelsall Av. L62 —2G 39
Kelsall Clo. L43 —4D 18
Kelsall Clo. L62 —2G 39
Kelvin Rd. L41 —3A 20
Kelvin Rd. L44 —4A 12
Kelvinside. L44 —4H 11
Kempson Ter. L63 —5F 27
Kempston St. L3 —3G 13
Kempton Rd. L62 —1H 27
Kendal Clo. L63 —3F 27
Kendal Clo. L66 —5D 46
Kendal Dri. L66 —5D 46
Kendal Rd. L44 —3E 11
Kendal St. L41 —1A 20
Kenilworth Ct. L65 —4C 48
(in two parts)
Kenilworth Dri. L61 —4A 24
Kenilworth Gdns. L49 —1E 17
Kenilworth Rd. L44 —2H 11
Kenilworth Rd. L64 —1C 42
Kenmore Rd. L43 —6C 18
Kennet Rd. L63 —4D 26
Kensington Gdns. L46 —5E 9
Kensington Rd. L65 —2G 47
Kensington St. L7 —3H 13
Kent Clo. L63 —3H 33
Kent Gdns. L1 —5F 13
Kentmere Dri. L61 —6B 24
Kent M. L43 —3F 19
Kent Pl. L41 —1H 19
Kentridge Dri. L66 —4D 46
Kent Rd. L44 —2E 11
Kent St. L1 —5F 13
Kent St. L43 —3F 19
Kenwick Clo. L66 —4C 46
Kenwyn Rd. L45 —6F 3
Kenyon Ter. L43 —2F 19
Kerry Croft. L66 —6E 47
Kestrel Av. L49 —1D 16
Kestrel Clo. L49 —1D 16
Kestrel Rd. L46 —5C 8
Kestrel Rd. L60 —4E 31
Keswick Av. L63 —1E 39
Keswick Gdns. L63 —6A 34
Keswick Pl. L43 —4B 10
Keswick Rd. L45 —4D 2
Kevelioc Clo. L63 —6F 27
Kew St. L5 —6F 5
Kiddman St. L9 —1H 5
Kilburn Av. L62 —5C 34
Killarney Gro. L44 —2E 11
Killington Way. L4 —3G 5
Kilmalcolm Clo. L43 —3D 18
Kiln Rd. L49 —4G 17
Kimberley Clo. L8 —6H 13
Kimberley Rd. L45 —5F 3
Kimberley St. L43 —5D 10
Kindale Rd. L43 —6C 18
Kinder St. L6 —2H 13
King Edward Dri. L62 —3H 27
King Edward St. L3 —3D 12
Kingfisher Way. L49 —1D 16
King George Dri. L44 —6G 3
King George's Dri. L62 —3H 27
King George's Way. L43 —6C 10
Kinglake Rd. L44 —1H 11
Kinglass Rd. L62 —6H 27
Kinglass Rd. L63 —6H 27
King's Av. L47 —5F 7
Kingsbrook Way. L63 —1E 27
King's Brow. L63 —3D 26
Kingsbury. L48 —5F 15
King's Clo. L63 —2D 26
Kings Ct. L47 —6C 6
Kings Ct. L63 —3D 26
Kingsdale Av. L42 —5H 19
Kings Dock Rd. L1 —6F 13
Kingsdown St. L41 —3A 20
King's Dri. L48 —2A 22
King's Dri. L61 —4B 24
King's Dri. N. L48 —6F 15
King's Gap, The. L47 —1C 14
Kingsland Rd. L42 —3G 19
King's La. L63 —2D 26
Kingsley Av. L62 —2G 39
Kingsley Clo. L61 —6C 24
Kingsley Rd. L44 —2F 11
Kingsley Rd. L65 —2A 48
Kingsley St. L41 —5E 11
Kingsmead Gro. L43 —2D 18
Kingsmead Rd. L43 —2D 18
Kingsmead Rd. L46 —3F 9
Kingsmead Rd. N. L43 —2D 18
Kingsmead Rd. S. L43 —2D 18
Kings Mt. L41 —3G 19
Kings Mt. L43 —3G 19
Kings Pde. L3 —5E 13
King's Pde. L45 —3B 2
King's Rd. L20 —1E 5
King's Rd. L63 —1D 26
Kings Rd. L66 —6C 40
Kings Sq. L41 —1B 20
Kingston Clo. L46 —5E 9
King St. L42 —6C 20
King St. L44 —6H 3
King St. L65 —1A 48
Kingsville Rd. L63 —4E 27
Kings Wlk. L42 —6C 20
Kings Wlk. L48 —5E 15
Kingsway. L44 —2B 12
(Second Mersey Tunnel)
Kingsway. L45 —5E 3
Kingsway. L60 —5E 31
Kingsway. L63 —2D 26
Kingsway Pk. L3 —1F 13
Kingsway Tunnel App. L44 & L45 —1C 10
Kings Wharf. L41 —4A 12

Kingswood Boulevd. L63
— 1E 27
Kingswood Rd. L44 —6G 3
Kington Rd. L48 —4C 14
Kinloss Rd. L49 —4C 16
Kinmel Clo. L41 —6H 11
Kinmel St. L8 —2H 21
Kinnaird Rd. L45 —5E 3
Kinnerley Rd. L65 —4G 47
Kinnerton Clo. L46 —5B 8
Kinross Rd. L45 —5B 2
Kinsey Rd. L65 —6B 48
Kintore Clo. L63 —1E 39
Kipling Av. L42 —6B 20
Kirby Clo. L48 —6E 15
Kirby Mt. L48 —1A 22
Kirby Pk. L48 —6E 15
Kirby Pk. Mans. L48 —6D 14
Kirk Cotts. L45 —4F 3
Kirkdale Rd. L5 —1F 5
Kirkdale Vale. L4 —4G 5
Kirket Clo. L63 —5G 27
Kirket La. L63 —5F 27
Kirkfield Gro. L42 —6C 20
Kirkland Av. L42 —5H 19
Kirkland Rd. L45 —4G 3
Kirklands, The. L48 —6E 15
Kirkmount. L49 —2G 17
Kirk St. L5 —5G 5
Kirkway. L45 —4F 3
Kirkway. L49 —3E 17
(Greasby)
Kirkway. L49 —2F 17
(Upton)
Kirkway. L63 —2D 26
Kitchen St. L1 —6F 13
Knap, The. L60 —5C 30
Knaresborough Rd. L44 —1D 10
Knight St. L1 —5G 13
Knoll, The. L43 —4E 19
Knottingley Dri. L66 —2C 46
Knowe, The. L64 —5C 38
Knowle Clo. L46 —4E 47
Knowles St. L41 —1H 5
Knowsley Clo. L42 —6C 20
Knowsley Ct. L42 —6C 20
Knowsley Rd. L42 —6C 20
Knowsley Rd. L45 —5E 3
Knowsley St. L4 —1H 5
Knox Clo. L62 —3H 27
Knox St. L41 —2D 22
Knutsford Grn. L46 —4E 9
Knutsford Rd. L46 —4E 9
Kronsbec Av. L66 —1D 46
Kylemore Clo. L61 —6A 24
Kylemore Dri. L61 —6A 24
Kylemore Rd. L43 —3E 19
Kylemore Way. L61 —6A 24

Laburnum Ct. L8 —3H 21
(off Weller Way)
Laburnum Farm Clo. L64
— 2E 43
Laburnum Gro. L61 —2H 33
Laburnum Gro. L66 —6B 46
Laburnum Rd. L41 —3G 19
Laburnum Rd. L43 —3G 19
Laburnum Rd. L45 —4F 3
Lace St. L3 —2F 13
Ladies Wlk. L64 —5C 36
Lad La. L3 —3D 12
Ladyewood Rd. L44 —2G 11
Laird Clo. L41 —6D 10
Laird Pl. L3 —1F 13
Laird St. L41 —5D 10
Lakeland Clo. L1 —6F 13
Lake Pl. L47 —6D 6
Lake Rd. L47 —5D 6
Lakeside Ct. L45 —3G 3
Lake St. L4 —4H 5
Lambert St. L3 —3G 13
(off Islington)
Lambert Way. L3 —3G 13
Lambeth Rd. L5 & L4 —4F 5
Lambeth Wlk. L4 —4F 5
Lambourne Clo. L66 —6A 46

Lamport St. L8 —2G 21
Lancaster Av. L45 —5F 5
Lancaster Clo. L5 —5F 5
Lancaster Clo. L62 —3H 27
Lancaster Gdns. L65 —4B 48
Lancaster St. L5 —5F 5
Lancaster St. L9 —1H 5
Lancaster Wlk. L5 —5F 5
Lance Clo. L5 —6H 5
Lancelyn Ct. L63 —6G 27
Lancelyn Precinct. L63 —6G 27
(off Spital Rd.)
Lancelyn Ter. L63 —5F 27
Lancers Croft. L66 —6E 47
Lancing Rd. L65 —3B 48
Landican La. L49 & L63 —6A 18
Landican Rd. L49 —2D 24
Landseer Av. L64 —6D 36
Landseer Rd. L5 —6H 5
Langdale Av. L61 —5B 24
Langdale Rd. L45 —4D 2
Langdale Rd. L63 —5E 27
Langfield Gro. L62 —6B 34
Langham St. L4 —3H 5
Langham St. L4 —3H 5
Lang La. L48 —4D 14
Lang La. S. L48 —5E 15
Langley Clo. L43 —6D 10
Langley Ct. L65 —4C 48
Langley St. L63 —1G 33
Langley St. L8 —1G 21
Langrove St. L5 —6G 5
Langsdale St. L3 —2G 13
(in two parts)
Langstone Av. L49 —4C 16
Langton St. L20 —1C 4
Langtry Clo. L4 —2F 5
Langtry Rd. L4 —2F 5
Lansdowne Clo. L41 —5E 11
Lansdowne Ct. L43 —5D 10
Lansdowne Pl. L5 —5H 5
Lansdowne Pl. L43 —5D 10
Lansdowne Rd. L43 & L41
— 5D 10
Lansdowne Rd. L45 —3D 2
Lanyork Rd. L3 —2D 12
Lapworth St. L5 —5F 5
Larch Ct. L8 —3H 21
(off Weller Way.)
Larchdale Clo. L66 —6A 46
Larch Gro. L43 —5C 10
Larch Rd. L42 —2G 19
Larchwood Clo. L61 —6B 24
Larchwood Dri. L63 —2F 27
Larcombe Av. L49 —2F 17
Larkhill Av. L49 —6G 9
Larkhill Way. L49 —6G 9
Larksway. L60 —3D 30
Larton Rd. L48 —4G 15
Latchford Rd. L60 —5D 30
Latham St. L5 —5F 5
(in two parts)
Latham Way. L63 —1H 33
Lathom Av. L44 —1F 11
Latimer St. L5 —5F 5
Laund, The. L45 —6D 2
Laurel Av. L60 —4D 8
Laurel Av. L63 —5E 27
Laurelbanks. L60 —2A 30
Laurel Dri. L44 —4C 38
Laurel Dri. L65 —5H 47
Laurelhurst Av. L61 —5C 24
Laurel Rd. L42 —1F 11
Laurels, The. L61 —2A 34
Laurelwood Dri. L66 —6E 47
Laurence Deacon Ct. L41
— 6G 11
Lavan Clo. L6 —2H 13
Lavan St. L6 —2H 13
Lavrock Bank. L8 —3G 21
Lawford Dri. L60 —3E 31
Lawns Av. L63 —5B 28
Lawns, The. L43 —6B 10
Lawton St. L1 —4F 13
Laxey St. L8 —1G 21
Laxton Clo. L66 —6A 46
Layton Av. L43 —5D 18

Leach Way. L61 —3G 23
Lea Clo. L43 —3C 18
Leadenhall Clo. L5 —5H 5
Leadenhall St. L5 —5H 5
Leafield Clo. L61 —3B 24
Leamington Clo. L64 —1C 42
Leamington Gdns. L49 —3H 17
Leander Rd. L45 —6E 3
Lea Rd. L44 —6G 3
Leas Clo. L66 —2C 46
Leasowe Av. L45 —5C 2
Leasowe Gdns. L46 —1E 9
Leasowe Rd. L46, L45 & L44
— 1D 8
Leasoweside. L46 —1G 9
Leas, The. L45 —4C 2
Leas, The. L61 —3D 24
Leather La. L2 —3E 13
Leaway. L49 —3D 16
Leawood Gro. L46 —5F 9
Ledbury Clo. L43 —5C 18
Ledsham Clo. L43 —3C 18
Ledsham Hall La. L66 —2F 45
Ledsham La. L66 —3G 45
Ledsham Pk. Dri. L66 —1A 46
Ledsham Rd. L66 —2H 45
Leece St. L1 —5G 13
Leeds St. L3 —2D 12
Lee Rd. L47 —5E 7
Lees Av. L42 —5B 20
Lees La. L64 —1E 43
Lees La. L65 —3B 48
Leeswood Rd. L49 —4G 17
Legh Rd. L62 —2H 27
Legion La. L62 —2B 34
Leigh Ho. L49 —1F 17
Leigh Pl. L1 —4F 13
Leigh Rd. L48 —4D 14
Leigh St. L1 —4F 13
(in two parts)
Leighton Av. L47 —5G 7
Leighton Chase. L64 —4B 36
Leighton Pk. L64 —5B 36
Leighton Rd. L41 —3A 20
Leighton Rd. L64 —2B 36
Leightons, The. L64 —5B 36
Leighton St. L4 —2G 5
Leison St. L4 —4F 5
Leiston Clo. L61 —2A 24
Lemon St. L5 —5F 5
Lennox Av. L45 —4F 3
Lennox La. L43 —4A 10
Leominster Rd. L44 —1F 11
Leonora St. L8 —3H 21
Leopold St. L44 —2A 12
Leslie Av. L49 —4D 16
Lester Clo. L4 —4G 5
Lester Dri. L61 —2G 23
Lestock St. L8 —6G 13
Leta St. L4 —2H 5
(in two parts)
Lethbridge Clo. L5 —5E 5
Letitia St. L8 —2H 21
Letterstone Clo. L6 —1H 13
Letterstone Wlk. L6 —1H 13
Levens Hey. L46 —5D 8
Leven St. L4 —3G 5
Leven Wlk. L65 —6G 41
Leven Wlk. L66 —6G 41
Lever Av. L44 —3H 12
Lever Causeway. L63 —4A 26
Leverhulme Ct. L63 —5G 27
Lever Ter. L42 —4A 20
Lewisham Rd. L62 —3A 28
Leyburn Rd. L45 —5D 2
Liberton Ct. L5 —5H 5
Lichfield Clo. L66 —6A 46
Lichfield St. L45 —4G 3
Liddell Ct. L45 —6B 2
Lightbody St. L5 —6D 4
Lightfoot Clo. L60 —4D 30
Lightfoot La. L60 —4D 30
Lighthouse Rd. L47 —1D 14
Lilac Gro. L66 —6B 46
Lillie Clo. L43 —5A 10

Lillyfield. L60 —5B 30
Lilly St. L42 —5C 20
Limbo La. L49 & L61 —1H 23
Lime Av. L63 —5D 26
Limehurst Gro. L62 —5B 34
Limekiln La. L5 —6F 5
Limekiln La. L3 & L5 —1F 13
Limekiln La. L41 —5H 11
Limes, The. L49 —2F 17
Lime St. L1 —3F 13
Lime St. L65 —6H 41
Lime Tree Clo. L66 —6B 46
Lime Tree Gro. L60 —3E 31
Linacre Ho. L20 —1E 5
Lincoln Clo. L45 —5G 3
Lincoln Gdns. L41 —5E 11
Lincoln Rd. L66 —4D 46
Lincoln St. L41 —5E 11
Linden Clo. L46 —4A 46
Linden Rd. L43 —6C 18
Linden Gro. L45 —4F 3
Lindens, The. L43 —2G 19
Lindeth Av. L44 —3F 11
Lind St. L4 —2H 5
Lindwall Clo. L43 —4A 10
Linear Ho. L46 —4C 8
Lingdale Av. L43 —1D 18
Lingdale Ct. L43 —6D 10
Lingdale Rd. L43 —6D 10
Lingdale Rd. L48 —4C 14
Lingdale Rd. N. L41 —6D 10
Lingham Clo. L46 —3D 8
Lingham La. L46 —2C 8
Links Av. L66 —6C 40
Links Clo. L45 —4D 2
Links Clo. L63 —5H 33
Links Hey Rd. L48 —3C 22
Linkside. L63 —2D 26
Linkside Way. L66 —6A 46
Links View. L43 —2C 18
Links View. L45 —3D 2
Links View. L66 —6C 40
Linksway. L45 —4D 2
Linnets Way. L60 —3A 30
Linton St. L4 —2H 5
Linwood Rd. L42 —4A 20
Lions Clo. L43 —1E 19
Lipton Clo. L20 —1E 5
Liscard Cres. L44 —6F 3
Liscard Gro. L44 —1E 11
Liscard Ho. L44 —1F 11
Liscard Rd. L44 —1F 11
Liscard Way. L44 —1F 11
Liscard Village. L45 —6F 3
Litcham Clo. L49 —6G 9
Litchfield St. L8 —6H 13
Lit. Canning St. L8 —6H 13
Lit. Catharine St. L8 —6H 13
Little Ct. L3 —1E 13
Littledale Rd. L44 —2H 11
Little Grn. L66 —4D 46
Lit. Hardman St. L1 —5G 13
Lit. Howard St. L3 —1D 12
Lit. Huskisson St. L8 —6H 13
Little La. L64 —4A 36
Littlemore Clo. L49 —2D 16
Lit. St Bride St. L8 —5H 13
Lit. Stanney La. CH2 —6G 48
Lit. Storeton La. L63 —3A 26
Littleton Clo. L43 —3C 18
Lit. Whissage. L66 —5F 47
Lit. Woolton St. L7 —4H 13
Liverpool Rd. L64 —5C 36
Liversidge Rd. L42 —3H 19
Liver St. L1 —5E 13
Livingstone Gdns. L41 —6G 11
Livingstone Rd. L46 —1G 9
Livingstone St. L41 —6G 11
Livingston Rd. L65 —2G 41
Llandaff Clo. L66 —6E 47
Llanrwst Clo. L8 —2G 21
Lloyd Av. L41 —6F 11
Lloyd Clo. L6 —1H 13
Lloyd Dri. L49 —4C 16
Lloyd Dri. L65 —6B 48
Lochinver Av. L66 —1H 45

Lochinver St. L9 —1H 5
Locker Pk. L49 —3C 16
Lock Rd. L62 —3E 35
Loddon Clo. L49 —6G 9
Lodge La. L62 —3H 27
Lodwick St. L20 —2D 4
Logan Av. L44 —4F 11
Logan Towers. L5 —6E 5
Lois Ct. L45 —5G 3
Lombard Rd. L46 —3F 9
Lombardy Av. L49 —5B 16
Lime Tree Gro. L60 —3E 31
London Rd. L3 —3G 13
Longacre Clo. L45 —6D 2
Longacres Rd. L64 —3C 36
Longfield Clo. L49 —3D 16
Long Hey Rd. L48 —2C 22
Longland Rd. L45 —5F 3
Longlooms Way. L66 —6D 48
Long Meadow. L60 —5B 30
Longridge Av. L49 —2E 17
Longridge Wlk. L4 —3G 5
Longsight Clo. L43 —2G 25
Longview Av. L45 —6E 3
Longville St. L8 —2G 21
Lonsborough Rd. L44 —2G 11
Lonsdale Av. L45 —5E 3
Looms, The. L64 —3A 36
Loomsway. L61 —3H 23
Loraine St. L5 —5H 5
Lord Nelson St. L3 —3G 13
Lords Av. L43 —5A 10
Lord St. L2 —4E 13
Lord St. L41 —6A 12
Loretto Dri. L49 —1G 17
Loretto Rd. L44 —6D 2
Lorne Ct. L43 —3F 19
Lorne Rd. L22 —3E 19
Lorn St. L41 —1A 20
Lothair Rd. L4 —4H 5
Lothian St. L8 —2H 21
Lough Grn. L63 —1G 33
Love La. L3 —1D 12
Love La. L44 —2E 11
Lowell St. L4 —4H 5
Lwr. Arkwright St. L5 —6G 5
Lwr. Bank View. L20 —2D 4
Lwr. Beau St. L5 —1G 13
Lwr. Castle St. L2 —4E 13
Lwr. Flaybrick Rd. L43 —5C 10
Lower Grn. L49 —4G 17
Lwr. Mersey St. L65 —2G 41
Lwr. Mersey View. L20 —2D 4
Lwr. Milk St. L3 —3D 13
Lower Rd. L62 —3H 27
Lwr. Thingwall La. L61 —3E 25
Lowfields Av. L62 —2F 39
Lowfields Clo. L62 —2F 39
Low Hill. L6 —2H 13
Lowry Bank. L44 —2A 12
Lowther St. L8 —6H 13
Lowwood Gro. L41 —2H 19
Low Wood Grn. L61 —5E 25
Lowwood Rd. L41 —2H 19
Low Wood St. L6 —2H 13
Loxdale Dri. L65 —4F 47
Lucerne Rd. L44 —3H 11
Ludlow Ct. L48 —6D 14
Ludlow Dri. L48 —6D 14
Ludlow Gro. L62 —2B 34
Ludlow St. L4 —2H 5
Luke St. L8 —1H 21
Luke St. L44 —3A 12
Lully St. L7 —5H 13
Lumley Rd. L44 —2H 11
Lundie Pl. L6 —6H 5
Lupus Way. L66 —4F 47
Luton Gro. L4 —3G 5
Luton Rd. L65 —2F 47
Luton St. L5 —6D 4
Lutyens Clo. L4 —3H 5
Luxmore Rd. L4 —2H 5
Lycett Rd. L44 —6C 2
Lydbrook Clo. L42 —4B 20
Lydden Rd. L65 —6H 41

Lydia Ann St. L1 —5F 13
Lydiate La. L64 —5A 38
Lydiate, The. L60 —4B 30
Lyle St. L5 —6E 5
Lymington Rd. L44 —1D 10
Lynas St. L41 —6H 11
Lyncroft Rd. L44 —3G 11
Lyndale Av. L62 —1G 39
Lyndhurst. L48 —4C 14
Lyndhurst Av. L61 —6C 24
Lyndhurst Rd. L61 —4C 24
Lyndhurst Rd. L45 —5D 2
Lyndhurst Rd. L47 —4G 7
Lyndhurst Rd. L61 —4G 23
Lyneal Av. L66 —4C 46
Lynnbank. L43 —3F 19
Lynndene. L66 —6D 40
Lynton Clo. L60 —5D 30
Lynton Dri. L63 —6G 27
Lynton Rd. L45 —5C 2
Lynwood Av. L44 —2E 11
Lynwood Dri. L61 —3A 24
Lyons Clo. L44 —4E 9
Lyons Rd. L46 —4E 9
Lytton Av. L42 —6B 20
Lytton St. L6 —2H 13

McAlpine Clo. L49 —1G 17
Macbeth St. L20 —2F 5
MacDona Dri. L48 —6D 14
Macdonald Dri. L49 —4D 16
Macdonald Rd. L46 —5C 8
McGarva Way. L65 —3A 48
McGregor St. L5 —6G 5
Mackenzie Clo. L6 —6H 5
Mackenzie Rd. L46 —2H 9
Mackenzie St. L6 —6H 5
Mackenzie Wlk. L6 —6H 5
McKeown Clo. L5 —6F 5
Maddock Rd. L44 —6H 3
Maddock St. L41 —5G 11
Maddrell St. L3 —1D 12
Madelaine St. L8 —1H 21
Madeley Clo. L48 —6D 14
Madeley Dri. L48 —6D 14
Maelor Clo. L63 —5H 33
Magazine Av. L45 —4F 3
Magazine Brow. L45 —4G 3
Magazine La. L45 —4F 3
Magazine Rd. L62 —6B 28
Magazines Promenade. L45
— 3G 3
Magdalen Ho. L20 —1F 5
Magnolia Clo. L66 —6F 47
Magnolia Wlk. L49 —5C 16
Magnum St. L5 —6E 5
Mahon Ct. L8 —6H 13
Maiden Gdns. L65 —4B 48
Main Rd. L62 —5H 27
Mainwaring Rd. L44 —2H 11
Mainwaring Rd. L62 —3B 34
Maitland Rd. L45 —3G 3
Major St. L5 —7G 4
Makepeace Wlk. L8 —1H 21
Makin St. L4 —1H 5
Malcolm Cres. L63 —5A 34
Malcolm Gro. L20 —2F 5
Maldwyn Rd. L44 —6F 3
Mallaby St. L41 —5E 11
Mallard Way. L46 —4C 8
Mallory Rd. L42 —5H 19
Mallory Rd. L65 —3G 47
Mallowdale Clo. L62 —6C 34
Malmesbury Clo. L49 —3C 16
Malpas Av. L43 —5E 19
Malpas Dri. L63 —2E 27
Malpas Gro. L45 —5E 3
Malpas Rd. L45 —5D 2
Malpas Rd. L65 —3F 47
Malta St. L8 —2H 21
Malvern Av. L44 —4A 48
Malvern Gro. L42 —5H 19
Malvern Rd. L45 —6B 2
Malwood St. L8 —3H 21
Manchester St. L1 —3F 13

Mandeville St. L4 —1H 5
Manesty's La. L1 —4F 13
Manfred St. L6 —3H 13
Manley Clo. L43 —4D 18
Manners La. L60 —5A 30
Mann Island. L3 —4D 12
Mann St. L8 —1G 21
Manor Clo. L20 —1G 5
Manor Clo. L64 —6A 36
Manor Dri. L46 & L44 —6F 9
Manor Flo. L66 —5D 46
Manor Hill. L43 —2E 19
Manor Ho. Flats. L62 —2B 34
Manor Ho., The. L49 —6F 9
Manorial Rd. L64 —5A 36
Manor La. L42 —5C 20
Manor La. L45 —6G 3
Manor La. L66 —4D 46
Manor Pl. L62 —2B 28
Manor Rd. L47 —5E 7.
Manor Rd. L61 —3H 23
Manor Rd. L62 —5B 34
Manor Rd. L62 —2H 31
Manor Rd. L63 —2H 31
Manorside Clo. L49 —1F 17
Mansfield Rd. L65 —5G 47
Mansfield St. L3 —2G 13
Manville Rd. L45 —4F 3
Maple Av. L66 —1C 46
Maple Gro. L62 —3A 34
Maple Gro. L66 —6G 47
Maples Ct L43 —4E 19
Maple St. L41 —2H 19
Mapleton Clo. L43 —6C 18
Maple Tree Gro. L60 —2E 31
Maplewood Gro. L43 —5C 10
Marathon Clo. L6 —1H 13
Marble Clo. L20 —1E 5
Marbury Gdns. L65 —1F 47
Marchwiel Rd. L65 —3B 48
Marcus St. L41 —6H 11
Mare Hall La. L64 —5F 37
Marfords Av. L63 —4A 34
Margaret Clo. L6 —1H 13
Margaret Rd. L4 —1G 5
Margaret's La. L66 —6H 39
Margaret St. L6 —1H 13
Marian Dri. L46 —5E 9
Maria Rd. L9 —1H 5
Marina Dri. L65 —2H 47
(in two parts)
Marina Wlk. L66 —3H 47
Marine Dri. L60 —4H 29
Marine Pk. L48 —3D 14
Marine Promenade. L45 —2F 3
Marine Rd. L47 —6C 6
Mariners Pde. L1 —4E 13
Mariners Pk. L44 —6H 3
(off Cunard Av.)
Mariners Rd. L45 —4G 3
Mariners Wharf. L3 —1E 21
Marine Ter. L45 —4G 3
Marion St. L41 —1A 20
Maritime Ct. L49 —6H 17
Maritime Grange. L44 —3A 12
Maritime Gro. L43 —2F 19
Maritime Pk. L43 —2G 19
Maritime Pl. L3 —2G 13
Maritime View. L42 —4H 19
Maritime Way. L1 —5F 13
Marius Clo. L4 —3H 5
Mark Av. L66 —3C 46
Market Pl. S. L41 —1B 20
Market Sq. L1 —4F 13
(off St John's Precinct)
Market St. L41 —1A 20
Market St. L47 —6D 6
Market St. L65 —3H 47
Market Way. L1 —4F 13
(off St John's Precinct)
Mark Rake. L62 —2B 34
Mark St. L5 —6G 5
Mark St. L44 —3A 12
Marks Way. L61 —5C 24
Marlborough Gro. L41 —3G 19
Marlborough Rd. L43 —3G 19
Marlborough Rd. L45 —4F 3

Marlborough Rd. L65 —4B 48
Marlborough St. L3 —2E 13
Marlborough Wlk. L65 —4B 48
Marlfield La. L61 —5C 24
Marline Av. L63 —4A 34
Marlowe Rd. L44 —1E 11
Marlowe Rd. L64 —5C 36
Marlston Av. L61 —3B 24
Marlwood Av. L45 —6C 2
Marmion Rd. L47 —6D 6
Marmonde St. L4 —3G 5
Marple Clo. L43 —4C 18
Marquis St. L3 —3G 13
Marquis St. L41 —3A 20
Marquis St. L62 —1H 27
Marsden Clo. L44 —6H 3
Marsden St. L6 —2H 13
Marsden Way. L6 —2H 13
Marshall Pl. L3 —1E 13
Marshall St. L41 —5G 11
Marsham Clo. L49 —6G 9
Marshfield Ct. L46 —2E 9
Marshlands Rd. L45 —5C 2
Marshlands Rd. L64 —2B 42
Marsh La. L63 —2C 26
Marsh St. L20 —2F 5
Marston Clo. L43 —5D 18
Marston Clo. L62 —2G 39
Marston Gdns. L65 —1F 47
Marten Av. L63 —4A 34
Martin Clo. L61 —3G 23
Martin's La. L44 —1G 11
Martlesham Cres. L49 —4B 16
Marwood Tower. L5 —5F 5
Marybone. L3 —2E 13
Maryland La. L46 —4D 8
Maryland St. L1 —5G 13
Maryville Clo. L65 —1A 48
Mason Av. L41 —3B 10
Mason Clo. L66 —5D 46
Mason St. L45 —3F 3
Massey Pk. L45 —6E 3
Massey St. L41 —5H 11
Mather Rd. L43 —2F 19
Mathew St. L2 —4E 13
Matthew St. L44 —3A 12
Maud St. L8 —1H 21
Maurice Jones Ct. L46 —4E 9
Mavis Dri. L49 —4G 17
Maxwell Clo. L49 —1G 17
Maxwell Clo. L65 —5G 47
May Av. L44 —3H 11
Maybank Rd. L42 —3H 19
Mayer Av. L63 —5F 27
Mayew Rd. L61 —3B 24
Mayfield Dri. L62 —2F 35
Mayfield Gdns. L44 —4C 26
Mayfield Rd. L45 —6D 2
Mayfield Rd. L63 —6G 27
Mayfields. L4 —3G 5
Mayfields N. L62 —2H 27
Mayfields S. L62 —2H 27
May Pl. L3 —4G 13
May Rd. L60 —3C 30
May St. L3 —4H 13
Mazzini St. L5 —6G 5
Meadfoot Rd. L46 —3D 8
Meadowbrook Rd. L46 —6D 8
Meadow Clo. L64 —1C 42
(Neston)
Meadow Clo. L64 —5B 38
(Willaston)
Meadow Cres. L49 —5H 17
Meadow Croft L60 —2E 31
Meadow Croft. L64 —5A 38
Meadowcroft Rd. L47 —4G 7
Meadowfield Clo. L42 —5B 20
Meadow La. L42 —5B 20
Meadow La. L64 —4A 38
Meadow La. L65 —1A 48
Meadow Rd. L48 —5H 15
Meadowside. L46 —1H 9
Meadowside Rd. L62 —4B 34
Meadows, The. L64 —1D 42
Meadow, The. L49 —5H 17
(in two parts)

Meadow Wlk. L61 —6A 24
Meadway. L45 —6E 3
Meadway. L49 —1H 17
Meadway. L60 —5B 30
Meadway. L62 —1A 34
Meadway. L66 —6B 40
Mealors Weint. L64 —4A 36
Meddowcroft Rd. L47 —4G 7
Medea St. L5 —5G 5
Medea Tower. L5 —5G 5
Medlock St. L4 —4F 5
Medowcroft Rd. L45 —5D 2
Medway Rd. L42 —5C 20
Melbourne St. L45 —3E 3
Melda St. L6 —2H 13
Melford Dri. L43 —6C 18
Meliden Gdns. L42 —3A 20
Melksham Dri. L61 —2H 23
Melling Rd. L45 —4G 3
Mellock Clo. L64 —1D 42
Mellock La. L64 —6D 36
Melloncroft Dri. L48 —1A 22
Melloncroft Dri. W. L48 —2A 22
Mellor Rd. L42 —5G 19
Melrose. L46 —4G 9
Melrose Av. L47 —6D 6
Melrose Dri. L66 —6A 46
Melrose Gdns. L43 —6D 18
Melrose Rd. L4 —3F 5
Melton Clo. L49 —2E 17
Melville Av. L42 —6C 20
Melville Pl. L7 —5H 13
Melville Rd. L63 —4E 27
Melville St. L8 —2H 21
Menai St. L41 —1G 19
Mendell Clo. L62 —3C 34
Mendip Clo. L42 —6G 19
Mendip Clo. L66 —4E 47
Mendip Rd. L42 —6G 19
Menlo Av. L61 —3B 24
Menlo Clo. L43 —3D 18
Menzies St. L8 —3H 21
Meols Clo. L66 —3E 47
Meols Pde. L47 —4E 7
Mercer Av. L44 —2E 11
Mercer Rd. L43 —5C 10
Mercer Wlk. L65 —3A 48
Mere Av. L63 —5H 33
Merebank. L3 —3C 18
Mere Clo. L66 —5D 46
Merecroft Av. L44 —3G 11
Mere Farm Gro. L43 —3D 18
Mere Farm Rd. L43 —3C 18
Mere Gro. L4 —2H 5
Mereheath. L46 —1E 9
Mere La. L5 —5H 5
Mere La. L45 —4C 2
Mere La. L60 —1A 30
Mere Pk. Rd. L49 —4C 16
Meriden Av. L63 —2G 33
Merlin Av. L49 —1D 16
Merlin Clo. L49 —1D 16
Merlin St. L8 —1H 21
Merrills La. L49 —2G 17
Merritt Av. L41 —5F 11
Merseybank Rd. L62 —1H 27
Mersey La. S. L42 —5C 20
Mersey Mt. L42 —4A 20
Mersey Rd. L42 —5C 20
Merseyside Ho. L1 —4E 13
(off Lord St.)
Mersey St. L44 —3A 12
Merseyton Rd. L65 —5H 41
Mersey View. L63 —3D 26
Merton Clo. L64 —2C 42
Merton Dri. L49 —4G 17
Merton Ho. L20 —1E 5
Merton Pl. L43 —1G 19
Merton Rd. L20 —1E 5
Merton Rd. L45 —6E 3
Merton Rd. L62 —2B 40
Merton Rd. L64 —2D 42
Merton Rd. L66 —4F 47
Mesham Clo. L49 —2F 17
Methuen St. L41 —5E 11
(in two parts)
Mews Ct. L64 —5B 38

Micawber Clo. L8 —2H 21
Michael Dragonetti Ct. L3
—1E 13
Middle Rd. L62 —3H 27
Midghall St. L3 —2E 13
Midland St. L43 —2G 19
Mile End. L5 —1F 13
Miles Clo. L49 —5C 16
Miles La. L49 —5C 16
Miles St. L8 —3H 21
Milford St. L5 —5D 4
Mill Bank. L64 —2E 43
Millbank Rd. L44 —2E 11
Millbrook Rd. L41 —3F 11
Mill Brow. L63 —3D 26
Millburn Heights. L5 —6G 5
Millbut Clo. L63 —3D 26
Miller Clo. L8 —3H 21
Millers Bri. L20 —1D 4
Millers Bri. Ind. Est. L20 —1D 4
Millers Way. L46 —5C 8
Millfield Clo. L63 —4D 26
Millfield Ter. L66 —6C 40
Mill Grn. L64 —5B 38
Mill Hey Rd. L48 —3B 22
Mill Hill. L43 —4E 19
Mill Hill Rd. L61 —1G 23
Millhouse Clo. L46 —4B 8
Millhouse La. L46 —4B 8
Millhouse La. L47 —4B 8
Millington Clo. L43 —6C 18
Mill La. L3 —3F 13
Mill La. L44 —2E 11
Mill La. L49 —4C 16
Mill La. L60 —3D 30
Mill La. L64 —6G 43
(Burton)
Mill La. L64 —2E 43
(Ness)
Mill La. L64 —4A 38
(Willaston)
Mill La. L66 —3D 46
Mill La. Ind. Est. L65 —6D 48
Mill Pk. Dri. L62 —2G 39
Mill Rd. L6 —1H 13
(in two parts)
Mill Rd. L61 —3C 24
Mill Rd. L62 —6B 28
Mill Rd. L63 —2D 26
Mill St. L8 —1G 21
Mill St. L42 —3H 19
Mill St. L64 —5B 36
Mill Ter. L43 —4D 26
Millthwaite Rd. L44 —1D 10
Mill View. L8 —2G 21
Mill View Dri. L63 —3D 26
Millwood. L63 —3D 26
Milman Clo. L49 —2F 17
Milman Rd. L4 —2H 5
Milner Cop. L60 —3C 30
Milner Rd. L60 —3C 30
Milner St. L41 —5E 11
Milnthorpe Clo. L4 —3G 5
Milton Cres. L60 —2C 30
Milton Pavement. L41 —1H 19
Milton Rd. L4 —1G 5
Milton Rd. L42 —3G 19
Milton Rd. L44 —4C 14
Milton Rd. L65 —3B 48
Milton Rd. E. L42 —4H 19
Minshull St. L7 —4H 13
Minster Ct. L7 —5H 13
Miranda Av. L63 —2C 27
Miranda Pl. L20 —2F 5
Miranda Rd. L20 —1F 5
Miriam Pl. L41 —5D 10
Miskelly St. L20 —3E 5
Miston St. L20 —3E 5
Mitylene St. L5 —5G 5
Mobberley Way. L63 —6G 27
Mockbeggar Dri. L45 —4C 2
Mockbeggar Wharf. L45 —4C 2
Modred St. L8 —2H 21
Moira St. L6 —3H 13
Mollington Rd. L44 —2G 19

Mollington St. L41 —2A 20
Molyneux Clo. L49 —2F 17
Molyneux Rd. L45 —3F 3
Mona St. L41 —6D 10
Monk Rd. L44 —1F 11
Monks Ferry. L41 —1B 20
Monks Gro. L65 —1H 47
Monk St. L5 —5H 5
Monk St. L41 —1B 20
Monks Way. L48 —5E 15
Monks Way. L62 —5F 27
Monmouth Rd. L44 —1D 10
Monro Clo. L8 —3H 21
Monro St. L8 —3H 21
Montgomery Hill. L48 —1D 22
Montpellier Cres. L45 —3E 3
Montpellier Ho. L45 —3E 3
Montrose Av. L44 —4A 12
Monument Pl. L3 —3G 13
Moorcroft Rd. L45 —6B 2
Moore Av. L42 —5A 20
Moorfield Dri. L64 —3A 36
Moorfields. L2 —3E 13
Moorings Clo. L64 —3A 36
Moorings, The. L41 —2H 19
Moorings, The. L60 —3G 29
Moorland Clo. L60 —4C 30
Moorland Rd. L42 —4A 20
Moorland Rd. L66 —5E 41
Moor La. L4 —1H 5
Moor La. L60 —3B 30
Moor Pl. L3 —3G 13
Moorside Av. L64 —5A 36
Moorside La. L64 —6A 36
Moor St. L2 —4E 13
Moorway. L60 —3D 30
Morecroft Rd. L42 —6C 20
Morello Dri. L63 —1H 33
Moreton Gro. L45 —5C 2
Moreton Rd. L49 —6E 9
Morland Av. L42 —6B 34
Morland Av. L60 —6D 36
Morley Av. L41 —6F 11
Morley La. L4 —6G 11
Morley Rd. L44 —2E 11
Morley St. L4 —6G 5
Morningside Rd. L20 —1E 5
Mornington Av. L65 —2A 48
Mornington Rd. L45 —5F 3
Morpeth Clo. L46 —4B 8
Morpeth Rd. L47 —2C 14
Morpeth Wharf. L41 —5A 12
Morris Ct. L43 —2D 18
Mortimer St. L41 —1B 20
Morton St. L8 —2H 21
(in two parts)
Mortuary Rd. L45 —5F 3
Morval Cres. L4 —1G 5
Mosedale Rd. L62 —1C 34
Moseley Av. L45 —1E 11
Moseley Rd. L63 —2G 33
Moses St. L8 —3H 21
Moss Clo. L64 —3C 42
Mossdene Rd. L44 —1D 10
Moss Gro. L42 —5F 19
Mosslands Clo. L66 —5E 47
Mosslands Dri. L45 & L44
—6C 2
Moss La. L42 —5F 19
Mossley Av. L62 —3B 34
Mossley Rd. L42 —4A 20
Moss St. L6 —3H 13
Moss Vale. L66 —5D 40
Mossy Bank Rd. L44 —1H 11
Moston Way. L66 —4F 47
Mostyn Av. L48 —6D 14
Mostyn Av. L60 —3G 29
Mostyn Clo. L4 —6G 5
Mostyn Gdns. L64 —4A 36
Mostyn Sq. L64 —4A 36
Mostyn St. L44 —2F 11
Mould St. L5 —5F 5
Mounsey Rd. L42 —4C 20
Mount Av. L60 —3B 30
Mount Av. L63 —2D 26

Mount Ct. L45 —3E 3
Mount Dri. L63 —2D 26
Mt. Farm Way. L66 —5C 46
Mount Gro. L41 —2G 19
Mt. Grove Pl. L41 —2G 19
Mt. Haven Clo. L49 —2G 17
Mt. Olive. L43 —4E 19
Mount Pk. L63 —2D 26
Mt. Pleasant. L3 —4G 13
Mt. Pleasant. L43 —4F 19
Mt. Pleasant Rd. L45 —5E 3
Mount Rd. L42 & L63 —1C 26
Mount Rd. L45 —3E 3
Mount Rd. L48 —6E 15
Mount Rd. L49 —2G 17
Mount St. L1 —6G 13
Mount, The. L44 —1G 11
Mount, The. L60 —3B 30
Mount, The. L63 —4G 27
Mt. Vernon Rd. L7 —3H 13
Mt. Vernon St. L7 —3H 13
Mt. Vernon View. L7 —3H 13
Mountway. L63 —2D 26
Mt. Wood Rd. L42 —1C 26
Mourne Clo. L66 —1A 46
Mudhouse La. L64 —5A 44
Mulberry Gro. L44 —2H 11
Mulberry Pl. L7 —5H 13
Mulberry Rd. L42 —5B 20
Mulberry St. L7 —5H 13
(in two parts)
Mulgrave Sq. L8 —6H 13
Mulgrave St. L8 —6H 13
Mulveton Rd. L63 —6F 27
Mumfords Gro. L47 —4G 7
Mumfords La. L47 —4F 7
Muncaster Clo. L62 —2B 34
Muriel St. L4 —2H 5
Murrayfield Dri. L46 —1F 9
Murray Gro. L48 —4C 14
Mynsule Rd. L63 —6F 27
Myrtle Gro. L44 —2H 11
Myrtle Pde. L7 —5H 13
Myrtle St. L7 —5H 13
Myrtle St. L65 —2G 41

Nairn Clo. L63 —1F 39
Nansen Gro. L4 —2H 5
Nant Pk. Ct. L45 —3G 3
Nantwich Clo. L49 —5G 17
Nantwich Rd. L64 —4F 47
Napier Dri. L46 —5F 9
Napier Rd. L62 —1H 27
Napier St. L20 —2D 4
Naples Rd. L44 —2H 11
Napps Way. L61 —1C 30
Naseby Clo. L43 —3A 18
Naseby St. L4 —1H 5
Nash Gro. L3 —2F 13
Naylor Ct. L66 —1E 47
Naylor Rd. L43 —5C 10
Naylor St. L3 —2E 13
Neale Dri. L49 —4E 17
Needham Cres. L43 —3B 18
Needwood Dri. L63 —6F 27
Nelson Ct. L42 —6C 20
Nelson Dri. L61 —5A 24
Nelson Rd. L42 —6C 20
Nelson Rd. L65 —2G 41
Nelson's Croft. L63 —6G 27
Nelson St. L1 —6F 13
Nelson St. L20 —1D 4
Nelson St. L45 —4G 3
Nelson St. L65 —2G 41
Neptune St. L41 —6H 11
Ness Acre La. L64 —5A 38
Neston Grn. L66 —3D 46
(in two parts)
Neston Rd. L63 & L64 —6H 31
(Neston)
Neston Rd. L64 —2D 42
(Ness)
Neston Rd. L64 & L66 —5A 38
(Willaston)
Neston St. L4 —2H 5
Netherby St. L8 —4H 21

Netherfield Clo. L43 —3A 18
Netherfield Rd. N. L5 —5G 5
Netherfield Rd. S. L5 —1G 13
Netherpool Rd. L66 —6F 41
Netherton Rd. L46 —5E 9
Netley St. L4 —3G 5
Neva Av. L46 —5D 8
Neville Clo. L43 —3A 18
Neville Rd. L44 —1E 11
Neville Rd. L62 —4C 34
Nevin St. L6 —2H 13
New Acres Clo. L43 —5A 10
Newark Clo. L43 —3A 18
Newark St. L4 —2G 5
New Bird St. L1 —6F 13
Newbold Cres. L48 —4G 15
Newbridge Clo. L49 —4H 17
New Bridge Rd. L65 —3D 48
Newburn. L43 —2F 19
Newburns La. L43 —4F 19
Newburn St. L4 —1H 5
Newby St. L4 —3H 5
New Chester Rd. L41, L42, L62 & L66 —2B 20
Newdales Clo. L43 —6A 10
Newell Rd. L44 —6F 3
New Ferry By-Pass. L62 —1H 27
New Ferry Rd. L62 —2H 27
New Grosvenor Rd. L65 —6H 41
New Hall La. L47 —1D 14
Newhall St. L1 —6F 13
Newhaven Rd. L45 —4G 3
New Hedley Gro. L5 —6E 5
New Henderson St. L8 —1G 21
New Hey La. L64 —6B 38
New Hey Rd. L49 —3H 17
New Houses La. L64 —3C 42
Newington. L1 —4F 13
New Islington. L3 —2G 13
Newland Dri. L44 —1E 11
Newlands Clo. L6 —1H 13
Newlands Rd. L63 —5H 27
Newlands St. L6 —1H 13
Newlands Wlk. L6 —1H 13
Newling St. L41 —6G 11
Newlyn Clo. L47 —3G 7
Newlyn Rd. L47 —3G 7
Newman St. L4 —3F 5
Newnham Dri. L65 —3A 48
Newport Av. L45 —4B 2
Newport Clo. L43 —3A 18
Newport Ct. L5 —6E 5
Newport St. L5 —5D 4
New Quay. L3 —3D 12
New Rd. L66 —5A 40
New School La. L66 —5B 40
Newsham St. L5 —6F 5
New St. L44 —3A 12
New St. L64 —2C 42
Newton Av. L49 —2F 17
Newton Cross La. L48 —5G 15
Newton Dri. L48 —5G 15
Newton Pk. Rd. L48 —5G 15
Newton Rd. L44 —1E 11
Newton Rd. L47 —5E 7
Newton Rd. L65 —2A 48
Newton St. L41 —6G 11
Newton Way. L3 —4H 13
Newton Way. L49 —2F 17
New Tower Ct. L45 —3G 3
Newtown. L64 —6D 36
New Way Bus. Cen. L44 —3H 11
Nicholas St. L3 —2F 13
Nicholls Dri. L61 —6B 24
Nicholson St. L5 —5G 5
Nickleby Clo. L8 —2H 21
Nickleby St. L8 —2H 21
Nicola Ct. L45 —5G 3
Nigel Rd. L60 —3E 31
Nimrod St. L4 —2H 5
Nixon St. L4 —1H 5
Noctorum Av. L43 —2A 18
Noctorum Dell. L43 —3B 18
Noctorum La. L43 —1B 18
Noctorum Rd. L43 —2C 18
Noctorum Way. L43 —3B 18
Nook, The. L43 —2F 19
Nook, The. L48 —5B 16
Norbury Av. L63 —4E 27
Norbury Clo. L63 —4F 27
Norbury Gdns. L42 —3A 20
Norfolk Clo. L43 —3A 18
Norfolk Dri. L48 —6E 15
Norfolk Rd. L65 —2A 48
Norfolk St. L1 —6F 13
Norgate St. L4 —4H 5
Norlands Ct. L63 —6A 20
Norley Av. L62 —2G 39
Norley Av. L65 —1F 47
Norman Clo. L66 —6A 46
Norman Rd. L44 —3A 12
Normanston Clo. L43 —3F 19
Normanston Rd. L43 —3F 19
Norman St. L3 —3H 13
Norman St. L41 —5D 10
Norris Clo. L43 —3A 18
Northbrook Clo. L8 —6H 13
Northbrooke Way. L49 —4G 17
Northbrook Rd. L44 —2H 11
Northbrook St. L8 —6H 13
Northbury Rd. L66 —6E 47
N. Cheshire Trading Est. L43 —1G 25
North Clo. L62 —1A 34
Northcote Clo. L5 —1H 13
Northcote Rd. L45 —5B 2
N. Dingle. L4 —3F 5
North Dri. L45 —3D 2
North Dri. L60 —4C 30
Northern Rise. L66 —3E 47
N. Hill St. L8 —2H 21
N. John St. L2 —3E 13
Northop Rd. L45 —5E 3
North Pde. L47 —6C 6
N. Park Ct. L44 —2A 12
Northridge Rd. L61 —4C 24
North Rd. L42 —4G 19
North Rd. L48 —5C 14
North Rd. L62 —1C 40
North St. L3 —3F 13
North Ter. L47 —4F 7
Northumberland Gro. L8 —2F 21
Northumberland St. L8 —2F 21
Northumberland Ter. L5 —5G 5
N. Wallasey App. L45 —6A 2
Northway. L60 —2F 31
Northways. L62 —6B 28
N. William St. L44 —3A 12
Northwood Rd. L43 —5D 18
Norton Dri. L61 —2G 23
Norton Rd. L48 —4C 14
Norton St. L3 —3G 13
Norville. L66 —6D 40
Norwich Dri. L49 —6G 9
Norwood Ct. L49 —4D 16
Norwood Rd. L44 —3F 11
Norwood Rd. L49 —3E 17
Nowshera Av. L61 —4B 24
Nuffield Clo. L49 —3F 17
Nun Clo. L43 —4F 19
Nurse Rd. L61 —3D 24
Nursery Clo. L43 —4F 19
Nursery St. L5 —5F 5

Oak Av. L49 —1D 16
Oak Bank. L41 —2G 19
Oakbank St. L44 —2G 11
Oak Clo. L46 —6D 8
Oak Ct. L8 —3H 21
(off Weller Way)
Oakdale Av. L44 —3H 11
Oakdale Dri. L49 —5C 16
Oakdale Rd. L44 —4H 11
Oakdene Av. L66 —2C 46
Oakdene Clo. L62 —6B 34
Oakdene Rd. L42 —4G 19
Oakenholt Rd. L46 —4E 9
Oakes St. L3 —3H 13
Oakfield Rd. L62 —3A 34
Oakfield Rd. L66 —5G 39
Oakfield Ter. L66 —5G 39
Oak Gro. L65 —4G 47
Oakham Dri. L46 —4B 8
Oakham St. L8 —1F 21
Oakland Dri. L49 —1G 17
Oaklands Dri. L61 —2C 30
Oaklands Dri. L63 —3G 27
Oaklands Ter. L61 —2C 30
Oakland Vale. L45 —3G 3
Oakleaf M. L43 —2B 18
Oaklea Rd. L61 —3B 24
Oakleigh Gro. L63 —3F 27
Oakmere Dri. L49 —3C 16
Oakmere Dri. L66 —6F 47
Oakridge Clo. L62 —1A 34
Oakridge Rd. L62 —1A 34
Oak Rd. L63 —2F 27
Oak Rd. L66 —4G 39
Oaks La. L61 —5C 24
Oaks, The. L62 —3A 34
Oak St. L65 —2G 41
Oakway. L60 —5D 30
Oak Tree Pl. L42 —4B 20
Oakwood Dri. L43 —5C 10
Oakworth Dri. L62 —2A 28
Oarside Dri. L45 —5E 3
Oatlands, The. L48 —6E 15
Oban Dri. L60 —3C 30
Oberon St. L20 —2E 5
Observatory Rd. L43 —5C 10
O'Connell Rd. L3 —1F 13
Odyssey Cen. L41 —5G 11
Oil Sites Rd. L65 —2H 41
Oil St. L3 —1D 12
Old Barn Rd. L44 —2E 11
Old Bidston Rd. L41 —5F 11
Old Chester Rd. L41, L42 & L63 —3A 20
Old Chester Rd. L66 —2D 46
Old Church Clo. L65 —2G 41
Old Church Yd. L2 —3D 12
Old Farm Clo. L64 —5C 38
Oldfield Clo. L60 —1A 30
Oldfield Dri. L60 —2H 29
Oldfield Farm La. L60 —1H 29
Oldfield Gdns. L60 —2A 30
Oldfield La. L48 —3A 16
Oldfield La. L60 —1H 29
Oldfield Rd. L45 —5D 2
Oldfield Rd. L60 —1H 29
Oldfield Rd. L65 —2H 47
Oldfield Way. L60 —1H 29
Old Gorsey La. L44 —3F 11
Old Greasby Rd. L49 —2F 17
Old Hall Dri. L65 —3H 47
Old Hall Rd. L62 —2C 34
Old Hall St. L3 —3D 12
Oldham Pl. L1 —4G 13
Oldham St. L1 —4G 13
Old Haymarket. L1 —3F 13
Old La. L60 —3F 31
Old Leeds St. L3 —3D 12
Old Marylands La. L46 —4E 9
Old Meadow Rd. L61 —6A 24
Old Mill Clo. L60 —4D 30
Old Post Office Pl. L1 —4F 13
Old Pump La. L49 —4C 16
Old Quay Clo. L64 —6A 36
Old Quay La. L64 —6B 36
Old Ropery. L2 —4E 13
Old School Clo. L64 —2D 42
Old Vicarage Rd. L64 —5C 38
Old Welsh Rd. L66 —2H 45
Old Wood Rd. L61 —5B 24
Olinda St. L62 —2H 27
Olive Cres. L41 —3A 20
Olive Dri. L64 —5C 36
Olive Mt. L41 —3A 20
Oliver La. L66 —3D 46
Olive Rd. L64 —5C 36
Oliver St. L41 —1H 19
Oliver St. E. L41 —1A 20
Olivia Clo. L43 —3A 18
Olivia M. L43 —3A 18
Olivia St. L20 —2F 5
Ollerton Clo. L43 —3A 18
Olney St. L4 —1H 5
Onslow Rd. L45 —3F 3
Onslow Rd. L62 —1H 27
Orchard Clo. L66 —6F 47
Orchard Ct. L41 —4B 20
Orchard Dri. L64 —2C 42
Orchard Grange. L46 —6C 8
Orchard Haven. L66 —6E 47
Orchard La. L66 —5A 40
Orchard Rd. L46 —4E 9
Orchard Rd. L65 —5G 47
Orchard, The. L45 —4E 3
Orchard Way. L63 —3D 26
Orchid Gro. L17 —4H 21
Orchil Clo. L66 —1A 46
O'Reilly Ct. L3 —1E 13
Oriel Clo. L2 —4D 12
Oriel Cres. L20 —2E 5
Oriel Lodge. L20 —1E 5
Oriel Rd. L20 —1D 4
(Bootle)
Oriel Rd. L20 —2E 5
(Kirkdale)
Oriel Rd. L42 —4A 20
Oriel St. L3 —2E 13
Orkney Dri. L65 —6B 48
Orlando Clo. L43 —3A 18
Orlando St. L20 —2E 5
Ormesby Gro. L63 —5G 33
Ormiston Rd. L45 —4F 3
Ormond M. L43 —3A 18
Ormond St. L3 —3E 13
Ormond St. L45 —6F 3
Ormond Way. L43 —3A 18
Orne Ct. L43 —3F 19
Orphan St. L7 —5H 13
Orrell Rd. L45 —4G 3
Orret's Meadow Rd. L49 —4H 17
Orrysdale Rd. L48 —4C 14
Orry St. L5 —6F 5
Orston Cres. L63 —1G 33
Ortega Clo. L62 —2A 28
Orthes St. L3 —4H 13
Orwell Rd. L4 —3F 5
Osborne Av. L45 —4F 3
Osborne Gro. L45 —5F 3
Osborne Rd. L43 —2F 19
Osborne Rd. L45 —4G 3
Osborne Vale. L45 —5G 3
Osmaston Rd. L42 —5E 19
Ossett Clo. L43 —3A 18
Oteley Av. L62 —3B 34
Othello Clo. L20 —2E 5
Otterburn Clo. L46 —5B 8
Oulton Clo. L43 —4C 18
Oulton Way. L43 —5C 18
Oundle Rd. L46 —4E 9
Ouse St. L8 —2H 21
Oval, The. L45 —5D 2
Oval, The. L65 —4A 48
Overchurch Rd. L49 —1E 17
Overdale Av. L61 —4F 25
Overdale Rd. L64 —4C 38
Overgreen Gro. L46 —4D 8
Overpool Gdns. L66 —4F 47
Overpool Rd. L66 —2E 47
Overton Clo. L43 —4D 18
Overton Rd. L44 —1F 11
Overton Way. L43 —4D 18
Owen Rd. L4 —3F 5
Owen St. L62 —3H 27
Oxford Clo. L66 —6A 46
Oxford Dri. L63 —5H 31
Oxford Rd. L44 —1G 11
Oxford St. L7 —4H 13
Oxford St. E. L7 —4H 13
Oxley Av. L46 —2H 9
Oxton Grn. L66 —3D 46
Oxton Rd. L41 —2G 19
Oxton Rd. L44 —2F 11
Oxton St. L4 —2H 5

Pacific Rd. L41 —6B 12
Paddington. L7 —4H 13
Paddock Dri. L64 —3B 36
Paddock, The. L46 —6C 8
Paddock, The. L49 —2H 17
Paddock, The. L60 —3E 31
Paddock, The. L66 —4D 46
Padstow Rd. L49 —4C 16
Pagett Clo. L43 —3B 18
Page Wlk. L3 —2G 13
Pagewood Clo. L43 —3B 18
Paignton Rd. L45 —5D 2
Painswick Rd. L66 —5E 47
Paisley Av. L62 —1G 39
Paisley St. L3 —2D 12
Palace Hey. L64 —2E 43
Palatine Rd. L44 —3H 11
Palatine Rd. L62 —2A 34
Paley Clo. L4 —4H 5
Pall Mall. L3 —2D 12
Palm Ct. L8 —3H 21
(off Weller Way)
Palmerston Rd. L44 —1D 10
Palmerston St. L42 —5B 20
Palm Gro. L43 —1F 19
Palm Gro. L66 —6G 47
Palm Hill. L43 —3F 19
Palmwood Clo. L43 —6C 18
Paltridge Way. L61 —5B 24
Pansy St. L5 —4F 5
Parade, The. L64 —4A 36
Paradise St. L1 —4E 13
Park Av. L44 —2H 11
Parkbridge Rd. L42 —4G 19
Parkbury Ct. L43 —4E 19
Park Clo. L41 —1G 19
Park Dri. L43 & L41 —6E 11
Park Dri. L65 —4H 47
Parkend Rd. L42 —4G 19
Parker St. L1 —4F 13
Parkfield Av. L41 —1H 19
Parkfield Dri. L44 —1F 11
Parkfield Dri. L65 —5G 47
Parkfield Pl. L41 —1H 19
Parkfield Rd. L63 —6G 27
Parkgate La. L64 —6G 31
Parkgate Rd. L64 —5B 36
Parkgate Rd. L66 —4D 44
Park Gro. L41 —2H 19
Park Hill Ct. L8 —3H 21
Park Hill Rd. L8 —3H 21
Parkhill Rd. L42 —5G 19
Parkhurst Rd. L42 —5G 19
Parkland Ct. L43 —5A 10
Parklands. L66 —2C 46
Parklands Ct. L49 —5G 17
(off Childwall Grn.)
Parklands Dri. L60 —5D 30
Parklands Gdns. L66 —1D 46
Parklands View. L66 —1D 46
Park La. L1 —5E 13
Park La. L47 —3A 8
Parklea. L66 —1D 46
Park Pl. L8 —1G 21
Park Rd. L8 —1H 21
Park Rd. L42 —4A 20
Park Rd. L44 —2G 11
Park Rd. L47 —4G 7
Park Rd. L48 —5C 14
Park Rd. L60 —2D 30
Park Rd. L62 —5D 34
(Eastham)
Park Rd. L62 —4H 27
(Port Sunlight)
Park Rd. L64 —5D 38
Park Rd. L65 —3A 48
(in two parts)
Park Rd. E. L41 —1G 19
Park Rd. N. L41 —6D 10
Park Rd. S. L43 —1F 19
Park Rd. W. L43 —6D 10
Parkside. L44 —2G 11
Parkside Clo. L63 —3G 27
Parkside Rd. L42 —4A 20
Parkside Rd. L63 —3G 27
Parkside St. L6 —2H 13
Parkstone Rd. L42 —4G 19
Park St. L8 —2G 21
Park St. L41 —1H 19
Park St. L44 —1G 11
Park St. L64 —5C 36
Park Vale. L64 —6C 36
Parkvale Av. L43 —1G 25
Park View. L62 —3A 34
Park Way. L8 —6H 13
(in two parts)
Parkway. L45 —4C 2
Park Way. L47 —4G 7
Parkway. L61 —2B 24
Parkway Clo. L61 —2B 24
Park W. L60 —4H 29
Parkwood Clo. L62 —2B 34
Parliament Clo. L1 —6G 13
Parliament Pl. L8 —6H 13
Parliament St. L8 —6F 13
Parliament Way. L66 —6A 46
Parnell Rd. L63 —1G 33
Parr Gro. L49 —3C 16
Parr's Rd. L43 —4F 19
Parr St. L1 —5F 13
Parry St. L44 —3H 11
Pasture Av. L46 —3E 9
Pasture Cres. L46 —3E 9
Pasture Rd. L46 —2D 8
Pastures, The. L48 —5H 15
Paterson St. L41 —1G 19
Paton Clo. L48 —4F 15
Patricia Av. L41 —4D 10
Patten St. L41 —5E 11
Patterdale Rd. L63 —6F 27
Paul Orr Ct. L3 —1E 13
Paulsfield Dri. L46 —6E 9
Paul St. L3 —2E 13
Paxton Rd. L43 —3B 18
Paxton Way. L43 —3B 18
Peach St. L7 —4H 13
Pearson Rd. L41 —3A 20
Pearson Rd. L42 —3A 20
Pear Tree Clo. L60 —2E 31
Peartree Way. L66 —6E 47
Peckforton Dri. L66 —4E 47
Pecksniff Clo. L8 —2H 21
Peebles Clo. L66 —2H 45
Peel Av. L42 —4B 20
Peers Wood Ct. L64 —2C 42
Pelham Rd. L44 —2E 11
Pemberton Clo. L64 —5C 38
Pemberton Rd. L49 —4H 17
Pembridge Ct. L65 —4C 48
Pembridge Gdns. L65 —4C 48
Pembroke Av. L46 —6E 9
Pembroke Ct. L41 —3B 20
Pembroke Dri. L65 —4G 47
Pembroke Gdns. L3 —3H 13
Pembroke Pl. L3 —3G 13
Pembroke Rd. L20 —1E 5
Pembroke St. L3 —3H 13
Pendennis Rd. L44 —2G 11
Pendle Clo. L49 —1E 17
Pengwern St. L8 —2H 21
Pengwern Ter. L45 —4G 3
Penistone Dri. L66 —2B 46
Penkett Ct. L45 —5G 3
Penkett Gdns. L45 —5G 3
Penkett Gro. L45 —5G 3
Penkett Rd. L45 —5F 3
Penmon Dri. L61 —6B 24
Penn Gdns. L65 —2H 47
Pennine Rd. L42 —6G 19
Pennine Rd. L44 —1D 10
Pennine Wlk. L66 —2B 46
Pennington Grn. L66 —4C 46
Pennington St. L4 —1H 5
Pennystone Clo. L49 —1D 16
Penrhos Rd. L47 —1C 14
Penrhyd Rd. L61 —4H 23
Penrhyn Av. L61 —3C 24
Penrhyn St. L5 —6F 5
Penrith St. L41 —2G 19
Penrose St. L5 —5G 5
Pensall Dri. L61 —1B 30
Pensby Clo. L61 —4C 24
Pensby Dri. L66 —3D 46
Pensby Hall La. L61 —1B 30
Pensby Rd. L60 & L61 —3B 30
Pensby Rd. L61 & L60 —4C 24
Pensby St. L41 —5G 11
Penstone Dri. L66 —2B 46
Pentland Av. L4 —2H 5
Penuel Rd. L4 —1H 5

Peover St. L3 —2F 13
Percival Rd. L65 —1H 47
Percy Rd. L44 —3A 12
Percy St. L8 —6H 13
Perrin Rd. L45 —6C 2
Perry St. L8 —1F 21
Peter Price's La. L63 —5E 27
Peter Rd. L4 —1G 5
(in two parts)
Peter's La. L1 —4F 13
Peter St. L1 —3F 13
Peter St. L44 —3A 12
Peterswood Ct. L64 —2C 42
Peterwood. L42 —6C 20
Petton St. L5 —5H 5
Peveril St. L9 —1H 5
Philips La. L66 —3C 46
Phillips St. L3 —2E 13
Phillips Way. L60 —3A 30
Pickerill Rd. L49 —4D 16
Pickering Rd. L45 —3F 3
Pickmere Dri. L62 —2H 39
Pickop St. L3 —2E 13
Pickwick St. L8 —1H 21
Picton Clo. L43 —3D 18
Picton Clo. L62 —2F 39
Pikes Hey Rd. L48 —2D 22
Pilgrim St. L1 —5G 13
Pilgrim St. L41 —1B 20
Pimhill Clo. L8 —1H 21
Pincroft Way. L4 —4F 5
Pine Av. L63 —6F 27
Pine Ct. L8 —3H 21
Pine Ct. L41 —1H 19
(off Byles St.)
Pinedale Clo. L43 —3B 18
Pinedale Clo. L66 —6A 46
Pinehey. L64 —4B 36
Pine M. L1 —6G 13
Pineridge Clo. L62 —1A 34
Pine Rd. L60 —2E 31
Pines, The. L63 —6H 27
Pinetree Av. L43 —3A 18
Pine Tree Clo. L46 —5F 9
Pinetree Ct. L45 —6D 2
Pinetree Dri. L48 —6F 15
Pine View Dri. L61 —1C 30
Pine Walks. L42 —6F 19
Pine Way. L60 —1A 30
Pinewood Dri. L60 —3D 30
Pinfold. L48 —3C 14
Pinfold La. L48 —3C 14
Piper's Clo. L8 —3H 29
Piper's End. L60 —3H 29
Piper's La. L60 —1G 29
Pitch Clo. L49 —3D 16
Pitt St. L1 —5F 13
Plane Tree Rd. L63 —5E 27
Plantation Dri. L66 —6E 41
Plantation Rd. L62 —2D 34
Planters, The. L49 —3C 16
Platt Gro. L42 —1G 27
Pleasant Hill. L8 —1F 21
Pleasant St. L3 —4G 13
Pleasant St. L20 —1D 4
Pleasant St. L45 —4F 3
Pleasant View. L20 —1D 4
Pleasington Clo. L43 —3C 18
Pleasington Dri. L43 —3C 18
Pleck Rd. L65 —5G 47
Plemston Ct. L66 —5F 41
Ploughmans Clo. L46 —6A 46
Ploughmans Way. L66 —6A 46
Plumer St. L41 —5E 11
Plumpton St. L6 —1H 13
Plumpton Wlk. L6 —1H 13
Plumpton Way. L6 —1H 13
Plymyard Av. L62 —5A 34
Plymyard Clo. L62 —6B 34
Plymyard Copse. L62 —6B 34
Poets Corner. L62 —4H 27
Poll Hill Rd. L60 —2B 30
Pollitt Sq. L62 —1A 28
Pomfret St. L8 —1H 21

Pomona St. L3 —4G 13
Pond View Clo. L60 —3E 31
Ponsonby Rd. L45 —6C 2
Pool Bank. L62 —2H 27
Poolbank Rd. L62 —2H 27
Poole Hall Ind. Est. L66 —5F 41
Poole Hall La. L66 —5E 41
Poole Hall Rd. L65 —1G 13
Poole Rd. L44 —6H 3
Pool La. L49 —5G 17
Pool La. L62 —4A 28
Pool St. L41 —6H 11
Pooltown Rd. L11 —6F 47
Poolwood Rd. L49 —3H 17
Poplar Av. L49 —2F 17
Poplar Ct. L8 —3H 21
(off Weller Way)
Poplar Dri. L5 —6H 5
Poplar Dri. L63 —5G 27
Poplar Farm Clo. L46 —1C 16
Poplar Gro. L42 —3H 19
Poplar Rd. L43 —3F 19
Poplar Ter. L45 —4F 3
Poplar Way. L4 —3F 5
Poplar Weint. L64 —5C 36
Porlock Clo. L66 —5D 30
Portal M. L61 —6B 24
Portal Rd. L61 —6B 24
Port Arcades, The. L65 —2A 48
Portbury Clo. L62 —3A 28
Portbury Wlk. L62 —3A 28
Portbury Way. L62 —3A 28
Port Causeway. L62 —5B 28
Porter St. L3 —1D 12
Portia Av. L63 —2E 27
Portia Gdns. L62 —2E 27
Portia St. L20 —2E 5
Portland Ct. L45 —2E 3
Portland Gdns. L5 —1E 13
Portland Pl. L5 —1G 13
Portland St. L5 —1E 13
Portland St. L41 —5E 11
Portland St. L45 —2E 3
Porto Hey Rd. L61 —4H 23
Portree Av. L43 —6B 34
Portside Ind. Est. L65 —1G 41
Portside N. L65 —5H 41
Portside S. L65 —1G 41
Poulton Bri. Rd. L41 & L44 —3E 11
Poulton Grn. Clo. L63 —1F 33
Poulton Hall Rd. L44 —2E 11
Poulton Hall Rd. L63 —4G 33
Poulton Rd. L44 —2E 11
Poulton Rd. L63 —6G 27
Poulton Royd Dri. L63 —1F 33
Pound Rd. L66 —6C 40
Powell St. L43 —5D 10
Power Rd. L42 —1G 27
Power Rd. L62 —2D 34
Pownall Sq. L3 —3E 13
Pownall St. L1 —5E 13
Premier St. L5 —6H 5
Prentice Rd. L42 —6A 20
Prenton Dell Av. L43 —1A 26
Prenton Dell Rd. L43 —6C 18
Prenton Farm Rd. L43 —1A 26
Prenton Hall Rd. L43 —6D 18
Prenton La. L42 —6F 19
Prenton Pk. Rd. L42 —4G 19
Prenton Rd. E. L42 —5G 19
Prenton Rd. W. L42 —5G 19
Prenton Village Rd. L43 —6D 18
Prenton Way. L43 —6B 18
Prentonwood Ct. L42 —6G 19
Prescot Row. L2 —3E 13
Prescot St. L7 —3H 13
Prescot St. L45 —3E 3
Prestbury Av. L43 —5C 18
Prestbury Clo. L43 —5C 18
Preston St. L1 —3F 13
Price's La. L43 —4C 18
Price St. L1 —5E 13
Price St. L41 —5F 11
Priestfield Rd. L65 —2H 47
Priestway La. L64 —6A 44
Primrose Ct. L45 —3F 3

Primrose Gro. L44 —3A 12
Primrose Hill. L3 —3F 13
Primrose Hill. L62 —3G 27
Primrose Rd. L41 —6D 10
Primrose St. L4 —3F 5
Prince Albert M. L1 —6F 13
Prince Edward St. L41 —6G 11
Prince Edwin St. L5 —1G 13
Princes Av. L8 —6H 13
Princes Av. L48 —5D 14
Princes Av. L62 —5C 34
Princes Boulevd. L63 —1D 26
Princes Gdns. L3 —2E 13
Princes Pde. L3 —3C 12
Princes Pavement. L41 —1A 20
Princes Pl. L41 —3A 20
Princes Rd. L8 —6H 13
Princes Rd. L65 —1F 47
Princess Rd. L45 —4F 3
Princes Ter. L45 —4F 3
Princes St. L2 —3E 13
Princes St. L20 —2D 4
Princesways. L45 —5E 3
Prince William St. L8 —1G 21
Priorsfield. L46 —5E 9
Priory Clo. L63 —6G 27
Priory Rd. L4 —3H 5
Priory Rd. L48 —5E 15
Priory St. L41 —1B 20
Priory, The. L64 —4C 36
Priory Wharf. L41 —1B 20
Pritt St. L3 —2G 13
Private Dri. L41 —4F 25
Probyn Rd. L45 —6C 2
Procter Rd. L42 —6C 20
Proctor Rd. L47 —1E 15
Progress Pl. L2 —3E 13
(off Stanley St.)
Promenade. L47 —5D 6
Promenade Gdns. L17 —4H 21
Prophet Wlk. L8 —2G 21
Prospect Rd. L42 —6F 19
Prospect St. L6 —3H 13
Prospect Vale. L45 —6D 2
Providence Cres. L8 —1G 21
Prussia St. L3 —3D 12
(off Old Hall St.)
Prussia St. L3 —3E 13
(off Pall Mall)
Puddington La. L64 —6H 43
(Burton)
Puddington La. L64 —6C 44
(Puddington)
Pudsey St. L3 —3G 13
Pugin St. L4 —4G 5
Pulford Av. L43 —5E 19
Pulford Rd. L63 —4F 27
Pulford Rd. L65 —3F 47
Pulford St. L4 —4H 5
Pullman Clo. L60 —3F 31
Pump La. L48 & L49 —2B 16
Pump La. L49 & L49 —2B 16
Pump Rd. L41 —5A 12
Purbeck Dri. L61 —2H 23
Pye Rd. L60 —3C 30
Pym St. L4 —1H 5
Pyramids, The. L41 —1H 19
Pythian St. L6 —2H 13

Quadrant, The. L47 —1D 14
(off Albert Rd.)
Quaker La. L60 —2A 30
Quakers All. L2 —3E 13
Quantock Clo. L66 —1A 46
Quarry Av. L63 —5F 27
Quarry Bank. L41 —2H 19
Quarrybank Pl. L41 —2H 19
Quarrybank St. L41 —2G 19
Quarry Clo. L61 —1B 30
Quarry La. L61 —3C 24
Quarry La. L20 —1F 5
Quarry Rd. L64 —4F 37
Quarry Rd. E. L60 & L61 —2A 30
Quarry Rd. E. L63 —5G 27

Quarry Rd. W. L60 —2A 30
Quayside. L64 —2B 42
Queen Anne St. L3 —2G 13
Queen Av. L2 —3E 13
Queen Mary's Dri. L62 —3H 27
Queen's Av. L47 —5F 7
Queens Av. L65 —4G 47
Queensbury. L48 —4F 15
Queensbury Av. L62 —2C 34
Queensbury St. L8 —2H 21
Queens Ct. L6 —4H 5
Queens Dock Commercial Cen.
L1 —6F 13
Queen's Dri. L43 —6E 19
Queen's Dri. L60 —3A 30
Queen's Dri. Walton. L4 —1H 5
Queens Gdns. L65 —2H 47
Queens M. L6 —6H 5
Queens Pl. L41 —3A 20
Queen Sq. L1 —3F 13
Queens Rd. L6 —6H 5
Queen's Rd. L20 —1E 5
Queen's Rd. L42 —6C 20
Queens Rd. L44 —2A 12
Queen's Rd. L47 —6C 6
Queens Rd. L66 —6C 40
Queen St. L41 —3A 20
Queen St. L45 —6F 3
Queen St. L65 —2G 41
Queensway. L41 & L3 —5C 12
(Mersey Tunnel)
Queensway. L45 —5E 3
Queensway. L60 —5E 31
Queens Wharf. L3 —6E 13
Queenswood Av. L63 —1E 27
Quigley St. L41 —3B 20
Quillet, The. L64 —6D 36
Quinesway. L49 —2G 17

Raby Av. L63 —5H 33
Raby Clo. L60 —4B 30
Raby Clo. L63 —4G 33
Raby Ct. L65 —4B 48
Raby Dri. L46 —6D 8
Raby Dri. L63 —4G 33
Raby Gdns. L64 —5C 36
Raby Gro. L42 —1D 26
Raby Gro. L63 —1D 26
Raby Hall Rd. L63 —5E 33
Raby Mere Rd. L63 —1F 37
Raby Pk. Clo. L64 —5C 36
Raby Pk. Rd. L64 —5C 36
Raby Rd. L63 —1F 37
(Raby)
Raby Rd. L63 —5A 32
(Thornton Hough)
Raby Rd. L64 —5C 36
Rachel St. L5 —1F 13
Raddle Wharf. L65 —2G 41
Radford Av. L63 —1H 33
Radley Dri. L63 —5H 31
Radley Rd. L44 —6D 2
Radleys Ct. L8 —1H 21
Radnor Av. L60 —4B 30
Radnor Dri. L45 —5G 3
Radnor Pl. L43 —1G 19
Radstock Rd. L44 —6C 2
Radway Grn. L66 —2E 47
Raeburn Av. L48 —4E 15
Raeburn Av. L62 —5B 34
Raeburn Av. L64 —6D 36
Raffles Rd. L42 —2H 19
Raffles St. L1 —6G 13
Railside Ct. L5 —6E 5
Railway Cotts. L47 —4F 39
Railway Rd. L42 —5D 20
Raines Clo. L49 —3E 17
Rainford Gdns. L2 —4E 13
Rainford Sq. L2 —4E 13
Rake Clo. L49 —3G 17
Rake Hey. L46 —5B 8
Rake Hey Clo. L46 —5C 8
Rake La. CH2 —6C 40
Rake La. L45 —6F 3
Rake La. L49 —3G 17
Rake M. L49 —3G 17

Rakersfield Ct. L45 —3G 3
Rakersfield Rd. L45 —3G 3
Rake, The. L62 —2B 34
Rake, The. L64 —6H 43
Raleigh Rd. L46 —1G 9
Raleigh Rd. L64 —4D 36
Raleigh St. L20 —2D 4
Ramsey Ct. L48 —6D 14
Randle Clo. L63 —1G 33
Randle Meadow. L66 —5F 47
Randolph St. L4 —4H 5
Ranelagh St. L1 —4F 13
Rankin St. L44 —3E 11
Rannoch Clo. L66 —4F 47
Rappart Rd. L44 —2H 11
Rashid Mufti Ct. L8 —1H 21
Rathmore Clo. L43 —4E 19
Rathmore Dri. L43 —3E 19
Rathmore Rd. L43 —3E 19
Ravenhill Cres. L46 —1F 9
Ravenscroft Rd. L43 —2G 19
Ravenswood Av. L42 —1F 27
Ravenswood Rd. L61 —1C 30
Rawcliffe Rd. L42 —2H 19
Raymond Pl. L5 —1F 13
Raymond Rd. L44 —2G 11
Raymond Way. L43 —3B 18
Raymond Way. L64 —6E 37
Reade Clo. L63 —2G 33
Reading Clo. L5 —4F 5
Reading St. L5 —4F 5
Reay Ct. L44 —2A 12
Rectory Clo. L42 —3H 19
Rectory Clo. L60 —4A 30
Rectory La. L60 —4A 30
Rectory La. L66 —6H 45
Rectory Rd. L48 —6D 14
Red Banks. L48 —3B 22
Redbrook Clo. L62 —5B 34
Redburn Clo. L8 —3H 21
Redcar Dri. L62 —6B 34
Redcar Rd. L45 —5B 2
Redcroft. L49 —4C 16
Red Cross St. L1 —4E 13
Redditch Clo. L49 —3C 16
Redfern St. L20 —3E 5
Redfield Clo. L44 —1H 11
Redford Clo. L49 —3C 16
Red Hill Rd. L63 —4B 26
Redhills M. L65 —1H 47
Redhouse Bank. L48 —4C 14
Redhouse La. L48 —4C 14
Red Lion La. L66 —6C 40
Redmere Dri. L60 —3E 31
Redmont St. L41 —3A 20
Red Pike. L66 —5D 40
Redstone Clo. L47 —5F 7
Redstone Dri. L60 —2G 29
Redstone Pk. L45 —3D 2
Redvers Av. L66 —3A 40
Redwood Ct. L8 —3H 21
(off Byles St.)
Redwood Dri. L66 —6F 47
Reeds Av. E. L46 —2F 9
Reeds Av. W. L46 —2F 9
Reeds Ct. L46 —3G 9
Reeds La. L46 —1F 9
Reedville. L43 —2F 19
Reedville Gro. L46 —3F 9
Reedville Rd. L63 —4F 27
Regal Clo. L46 —6E 47
Regal Wlk. L4 —4G 5
Regent Rd. L20 —1C 4
Regent Rd. L45 —5B 2
Regents Clo. L61 —3D 24
Regent St. L3 —1D 12
Regent St. L65 —2F 47
Regents Way. L63 —1D 26
Reid Ct. L66 —6C 40
Rendal Clo. L5 —6H 5
Rendelsham Clo. L49 —2E 17
Rendel St. L41 —6H 11
Renfrew Av. L62 —6C 34
Renfrew St. L7 —3H 13
Renshaw St. L1 —4G 13
Repton Rd. L65 —3B 48
Reservoir Rd. L42 —6F 19

Reservoir Rd. N. L42 —6F 19
Reservoir St. L6 —1H 13
Rest Hill Rd. L63 —4B 26
Retail Mkt. L1 —4F 13
(off St John's Precinct)
Rhodeway. L60 —4D 30
Rhona Clo. L63 —1E 39
Rhuddlan Ct. L65 —5B 48
Rhyl St. L8 —2H 21
Ribbledale. L65 —4H 47
Ribblesdale Clo. L62 —6D 34
Ribble St. L41 —4D 10
Rice Hey Rd. L44 —6G 3
Rice La. L9 —1H 5
Rice La. L44 —6G 3
Rice St. L1 —5G 13
Richard Allen Way. L5 —1G 13
Richard Chubb Dri. L44 —5H 3
Richardson Rd. L42 —1E 27
Richmond Clo. L63 —3G 27
Richmond Ct. L65 —4B 48
Richmond Rd. L45 —2F 3
Richmond Rd. L63 —3F 27
Richmond Row. L3 —2G 13
Richmond St. L1 —4F 13
Richmond Way. L61 —1B 30
(Heswall)
Richmond Way. L61 —3C 24
(Thingwall)
Rich View. L43 —4F 19
Rickaby Clo. L63 —3A 34
Rickman St. L4 —3F 5
Ridgefield Rd. L61 —4B 24
Ridgemere Rd. L61 —4B 24
Ridge, The. L60 —1H 29
Ridgeview Rd. L43 —2B 18
Ridgeway, The. L47 —6G 7
Ridgeway, The. L60 —4D 30
Ridgeway, The. L63 —2B 18
Ridgewood Dri. L61 —5A 24
Ridings Hey. L43 —3B 18
Ridings, The. L43 —2B 18
Riding St. L3 —3G 13
Ridley Gro. L48 —4C 14
Ridley St. L43 —2G 19
Rigby Dri. L49 —5D 16
Rigby St. L3 —3D 12
Rimmer St. L3 —3G 13
Ringway. L64 —4C 36
Ringway. L63 —3E 47
Ringways. L62 —6B 28
Ringwood. L43 —4E 19
Ripon Av. L66 —2C 46
Ripon Rd. L45 —5C 2
Ripon St. L4 —2F 5
Ripon St. L41 —3A 20
Rishton Clo. L5 —6H 5
Rivacre Brow. L66 —6E 41
Rivacre Bus. Cen. L66 —2E 47
Rivacre Rd. L62, L65 & L66
—6E 35
Riva La. L60 —1A 30
Riverbank Clo. L60 —5B 30
Riverbank Rd. L60 —5A 30
River Gro. L62 —1H 27
Riverdale Rd. L44 —1H 11
Riversdale Rd. L48 —5C 14
River Side. L48 —6D 14
Riverside. L62 —4H 27
Riverside Bus. Pk. L8 —4H 21
Riverside St. L8 —5H 21
Riverside Wlk. L3 —5D 12
Riverside Wlk. L64 —2B 42
Riverside Walkway. L3 —5D 12
River View. L62 —1A 28
Riverview Rd. L44 —2A 12
Riverview Rd. L64 —2D 42
Riverview Wlk. L8 —3H 21
Riviera Dri. L42 —6H 19
Rivington Av. L43 —3C 18
Rivington Rd. L44 —2H 11
Rivington Rd. L65 —2A 48
Robert Dri. L49 —4E 17
Robertson St. L8 —2G 21
Roberts St. L3 —2D 12
Robert St. L41 —6H 11
Robins Croft. L66 —5F 47

Robin Way. L49 —5H 17
Robsart St. L5 —6G 5
Robson St. L5 —4H 5
Rochester Dri. L65 —5B 48
Rochester Rd. L42 —5C 20
Rock Av. L60 —2B 30
Rock Clo. L42 —5B 20
Rock Cotts. L45 —4F 3
Rock Farm Clo. L64 —1E 43
Rock Farm Dri. L64 —1E 43
Rock Farm Gro. L64 —1E 43
Rock Ferry By-Pass. L42
—4C 20
Rockfield Rd. L4 —4H 5
Rockland Rd. L45 —4D 2
Rocklands Av. L63 —2G 27
Rocklands La. L63 —4C 32
Rock La. E. L42 —6C 20
Rock La. W. L42 —1F 27
Rocklee Gdns. L14 —1E 43
Rockley St. L4 —3G 5
(in two parts)
Rock Pk. L42 —5C 20
(in two parts)
Rock Pk. Rd. L42 —6D 20
Rockpoint Av. L45 —4G 3
Rock View. L5 —5G 5
Rockville St. L42 —5B 20
Rockybank Rd. L42 —4H 19
Rocky La. L60 —3B 30
Rocky La. S. L60 —3C 30
Roderick St. L4 —1H 5
Roderick St. L3 —2G 13
Rodney St. L1 —5G 13
Rodney St. L20 —1D 4
Rodney St. L41 —2A 20
Roe All. L1 —4F 13
Roften Works Ind. Est. L66
—5F 39
Rokeby Clo. L3 —2G 13
Rokeby St. L3 —2G 13
Roker Av. L44 —2E 11
Roland Av. L63 —2D 26
Rolleston Dri. L45 —4D 2
Rolleston Rd. L63 —5G 27
Rollo St. L4 —4F 5
Roman Ct. L64 —6D 36
Roman Rd. L43 —1A 26
Roman Rd. L47 —4F 7
Romiley Rd. L66 —1E 47
Romilly St. L41 —1A 20
Romley St. L4 —1H 5
Romney Clo. L64 —6C 36
Romney Croft. L64 —6D 36
Romney Way. L64 —6D 36
Ronaldsway. L49 —1F 17
Ronaldsway. L60 —5B 8
Rone Clo. L46 —5D 8
Rooks Way. L60 —3A 30
Roper St. L8 —3H 21
Ropewalk, The. L64 —4A 36
Rosalind Av. L63 —2F 27
Rosalind Way. L20 —2F 5
Rosclare Clo. L43 —3B 18
Rosclare Dri. L45 —6D 2
Roscoe La. L1 —5G 13
Roscoe Pl. L1 —4G 13
Roscoe St. L1 —5G 13
Roscommon St. L5 —1G 13
(in two parts)
Roscote Clo. L60 —4B 30
Roscote, The. L60 —4B 30
Roseacre. L48 —4C 14
Roseberry Av. L44 —1G 11
Rosebery Gro. L42 —5F 19
Rosebery St. L8 —6H 13
Rosebrae Ct. L41 —6B 12
Rose Ct. L41 —1H 19
Rosecroft St. L47 —1C 14
Rosedale Rd. L42 —4A 20
Rosefield Av. L63 —2E 27
Rose Gdns. L64 —1D 42
Rose Hill. L3 —2F 13
Roselands Ct. L42 —6A 20
Rosemary Clo. L43 —5C 10

Rosemead Av. L61 —5B 24
Rose Mt. L43 —4F 19
Rose Mt. Clo. L43 —4E 19
Rose Mt. Dri. L45 —5E 3
Rose Pl. L3 —2F 13
(in two parts)
Rose Pl. L42 —4B 20
Rose St. L1 —3F 13
Rose Vale. L5 —6G 5
(in two parts)
Rosewood Dri. L46 —5B 8
Roslin Rd. L43 —3F 19
Roslin Rd. L61 —3H 23
Roslyn St. L42 —4B 20
Rossall Gro. L66 —1D 46
Rossall Rd. L44 —4F 5
Ross Av. L46 —1A 10
Rossbank Rd. L65 —6G 41
Rosscliffe Rd. L65 —6G 41
Ross Dri. L66 —2C 46
Rossendale Clo. L43 —3B 18
Rossfield Rd. L65 —6G 41
Rosslyn Cres. L46 —6E 9
Rosslyn St. L42 —5B 20
Rosslyn Pk. L46 —6E 9
Rossmore Gdns. L66 —1D 46
Rossmore Ind. Pk. L65 —1G 47
Rossmore Rd. E. L65 —6F 41
Rossmore Rd. W. L66 —6D 40
Rossmore Trading Est. L65
—6G 41
Rossmount Rd. L65 —1G 47
Ross Rd. L65 —1G 47
Ross Tower Ct. L45 —3G 3
Rosswood Rd. L65 —1G 47
Rostherne Av. L44 —2E 11
Rostherne Av. L66 —3E 47
Rothbury Clo. L46 —5C 8
Rothesay Clo. L65 —6G 41
Rotherwood Clo. L63 —3D 26
Rothesay Ct. L63 —5F 27
Rothesay Dri. L62 —1G 39
Rothesay Gdns. L43 —6D 18
Rothsay Clo. L5 —1G 13
Rotunda St. L5 —6F 5
Rowan Ct. L49 —5B 16
Rowan Gro. L63 —5E 27
Rowan Tree Clo. L49 —4C 16
Rowson St. L47 —6H 3
Rowton Clo. L43 —4D 18
Roxborough Rd. L66 —2H 45
Roxburgh Av. L42 —5H 19
Roxburgh St. L20 & L4 —1G 5
Royal Mail St. L3 —4G 13
Royal Shopping Arc., The. L64
—6C 36
Royal St. L4 —4G 5
Royal, The. L47 —3B 14
Royden Av. L44 —6H 3
Royden Rd. L49 —1E 17
(in two parts)
Royden St. L8 —3H 21
Royden Way. L3 —4G 21
Royston Av. L44 —6H 11
Royston Clo. L66 —4F 47
Rubbing Stone. L48 —3B 22
Ruby St. L8 —4H 21
Rudd St. L47 —6D 6
Rudgrave Clo. L43 —3B 18
Rudgrave M. L44 —6H 3
Rudgrave Pl. L44 —6H 3
Rudgrave Sq. L44 —6H 3
Rudstone Clo. L66 —2B 46
Rufford Rd. L44 —2G 11
Rugby Rd. L42 —5H 19
Rugby Rd. L65 —4A 48
Rugby Wlk. L65 —4B 48
Rullerton Rd. L44 —1E 11
Rumford Pl. L3 —3D 12
Rumford St. L2 —3D 12
Rumney Pl. L4 —3F 5
Rumney Rd. L4 —3F 5
Rundle St. L41 —5E 11
Runnel, The. L64 —1B 36
Ruskin Av. L42 —6A 20
Ruskin Av. L44 —2E 11
Ruskin Dri. L65 —4B 48

Ruskin St. L4 —2G 5
Rusland Av. L61 —5B 24
Russell Rd. L42 —4C 20
(in two parts)
Russell Rd. L44 —6C 2
Russell St. L3 —3G 13
Russell St. L41 —6A 12
Ruthin Clo. L65 —4B 48
Rutland Clo. L5 —6G 5
Rutter St. L8 —2G 21
Rycroft Rd. L46 —5B 8
Rycroft Rd. L47 —5G 7
Rydal Av. L43 —2E 19
Rydal Bank. L44 —1G 11
Rydal Bank. L63 —2G 27
Rydal Clo. L61 —5B 24
Rydal Clo. L64 —1D 42
Rydal Dri. L65 —5A 48
Rydal St. L5 —5H 5
Ryecroft Rd. L60 —4E 31
Ryland Pk. L61 —4C 24
Rylands Hey. L49 —3D 16
Ryleys Gdns. L2 —3E 13
(off Tempest Hey)
Rymer Gro. L4 —2H 5

S

St Agnes Rd. L4 —3F 5
St Aidan's Ct. L43 —1D 18
St Aidans Ter. L5 —5F 5
(off Latham St.)
St Aidan's Ter. L43 —1D 18
St Albans Ct. L5 —6E 5
St Albans Rd. L20 —1E 5
St Albans Rd. L43 —6E 11
St Albans Rd. L44 —2E 11
St Alban's Sq. L20 —1E 5
St Ambrose Way. L5 —1G 13
St Andrews Gdns. L3 —3G 13
St Andrew's Rd. L43 —1F 19
St Andrews Rd. L63 —2F 27
St Andrew's Rd. L65 —4B 48
St Andrew St. L3 —4G 13
St Annes Clo. L41 —6H 11
St Annes Gro. L41 —6G 11
St Anne's Ho. L20 —1F 5
St Annes Pl. L41 —6G 11
St Annes Ter. L41 —6G 11
St Anne St. L3 —3G 13
St Anne St. L41 —5G 11
(in three parts)
St Anne Way. L41 —6H 11
St Anthony's Pl. L5 —6F 5
St Asaph Rd. L66 —6A 46
St Augustine St. L5 —6F 5
St Austell Clo. L46 —4B 8
St Austells Rd. L4 —1G 5
St Bride's Rd. L44 —6H 3
St Bride St. L8 —5H 13
St Bridget's La. L48 —6D 14
St Brigids Cres. L5 —6E 5
St Catherines Gdns. L42
—3H 19
St Catherine's Rd. L20 —1E 5
St Columbas La. L44 —6H 3
St Crysostom's Way. L6 —1H 13
St David Rd. L43 —1E 19
St David Rd. L62 —5E 35
St Davids Dri. L66 —6A 46
St David's La. L43 —2B 18
St Domingo Gro. L5 —5H 5
St Domingo Rd. L5 —6G 5
St Domingo Vale. L5 —5H 5
St Edmond's Rd. L20 —1E 5
St Edmund's Rd. L42 —4F 27
St Edwards Clo. L41 —5F 11
St Elmo Rd. L44 —6H 3
St George's Av. L42 —5H 19
St Georges Av. L66 —6A 46
St George's Ct. L45 —6F 3
St Georges Gro. L46 —5D 8
St Georges Heights. L5 —6G 5
St George's Hill. L5 —6G 5
St George's Mt. L45 —3F 3
St George's Pk. L45 —3F 3
St George's Pl. L1 —3F 13
St George's Rd. L45 —5C 2

St George's Way. L1 —4F 13
(off St John's Precinct)
St George's Way. L63 —4A 32
St Gerards Clo. L5 —5F 5
St Helen's Clo. L43 —1F 19
St Hilary Brow. L44 —1D 10
St Hilary Dri. L44 —6D 2
St Hilary Dri. L45 —6D 2
St Hugh's Clo. L43 —1F 19
St Ives Ct. L43 —6E 11
St Ives Rd. L43 —1E 19
St James Ct. L45 —3F 3
St James Dri. L45 —3F 3
St James Rd. L41 & L43
—5D 10
St James Rd. L45 —3F 3
St James St. L1 —6F 13
St John's Clo. L47 —5F 7
St John's Ho. L20 —1E 5
St John's La. L1 —3F 13
St John's Pavement. L41
—1H 19
St John's Precinct. L1 —4F 13
St John's Rd. L20 —1D 4
St John's Rd. L45 —6C 2
St John's Rd. L65 —6E 35
St John's Sq. L1 —4F 13
(off St John's Precinct)
St John's Ter. L20 —1D 4
St John St. L41 —1H 19
St Johns Way. L1 —4F 13
St Josephs Cres. L3 —2F 13
St Kilda's Rd. L48 —6D 14
St Lawrence Clo. L8 —3H 21
St Lucia Rd. L44 —6H 3
St Lukes Pl. L1 —5G 13
St Margaret's Rd. L47 —1C 14
St Marks Cres. L46 —6A 46
St Martins Dri. L66 —5D 46
St Martin's Ho. L20 —1E 5
St Martins M. L5 —1G 13
St Mary's Av. L44 —1F 11
St Mary's Ct. L49 —3G 17
St Mary's Ga. L41 —1B 20
St Mary's Gro. L4 —1H 5
St Mary's La. L4 —1H 5
St Mary's Pl. L4 —1H 5
St Mary's St. L44 —1F 11
St Michael's Gro. L46 —5D 8
St Nathaniels St. L8 —5H 13
St Nicholas Pl. L3 —4D 12
(in two parts)
St Nicholas' Rd. L45 —6B 2
St Oswald's Av. L43 —4A 10
St Oswald's M. L43 —4A 10
St Paul's Av. L44 —3A 12
St Paul's Clo. L42 —5B 20
St Pauls Gdns. L66 —6B 40
St Paul's Pl. L20 —1F 5
St Paul's Rd. L42 —5B 20
St Paul's Rd. L44 —3H 11
St Paul's Sq. L3 —3D 12
St Paul's Vs. L42 —5B 20
St Peters Clo. L60 —4B 30
St Peter's Ct. L42 —6C 20
St Peter's Ho. L20 —1F 5
St Peter's Rd. L42 —6D 20
St Peter's Rd. L42 —6C 20
St Peter's Way. L43 —3A 18
St Saviour's Sq. L8 —5H 13
St Seiriol Gro. L43 —1E 19
St Stephens Clo. L60 —5E 31
St Stephen's Ct. L42 —6D 20
St Stephen's Pl. L3 —2F 13
St Stephen's Rd. L42 —5B 20
St Vincent Rd. L43 —1E 19
St Vincent Rd. L44 —6H 3
St Vincent St. L3 —5F 13
St Vincent Way. L3 —3G 13
St Werburghs Sq. L41 —1A 20
St Winifred Rd. L45 —4F 3
Saker St. L4 —4H 5
Salacre Clo. L49 —3H 17
Salacre Cres. L49 —3G 17
Salacre La. L49 —2A 18

Salacre Ter. L49 —2G 17
Salem View. L43 —4F 19
Salisbury Av. L48 —5C 14
Salisbury Clo. L66 —6A 46
Salisbury Dri. L62 —2H 27
Salisbury Rd. L5 —5H 5
Salisbury Rd. L45 —3E 3
Salisbury St. L3 —1G 13
(in two parts)
Salisbury St. L41 —2H 19
Salop St. L4 —1H 5
Saltburn Rd. L45 —6B 2
(in two parts)
Saltersgate. L66 —5F 47
Salthouse Quay. L3 —5E 13
Saltney St. L3 —6D 4
Samaria Av. L62 —2A 28
Sandalwood Dri. L43 —3B 18
Sandbeck St. L8 —4H 21
Sandbourne. L46 —5G 9
Sandbrook Ct. L46 —5E 9
Sandbrook La. L46 —5E 9
Sandcliffe Rd. L45 —3C 2
Sandfield Av. L47 —4F 7
Sandfield Clo. L63 —3D 26
Sandfield Pk. L60 —3H 29
Sandfield Rd. L20 —1F 5
Sandfield Rd. L49 —6H 17
Sandfield Rd. L63 —3D 26
Sandfield Ter. L45 —4F 3
Sandford St. L41 —6A 12
Sandham Gro. L60 —3E 31
Sandhey Rd. L47 —4E 7
Sandheys. L64 —4A 36
Sandheys Clo. L4 —4G 5
Sandheys Dri. L45 —4F 3
Sandhills Bus. Pk. L5 —4E 5
Sandhills La. L5 —4D 4
Sandhills, The. L46 —2E 9
Sandhills View. L45 —6B 2
Sandino St. L8 —1G 21
Sandiway. L47 —4F 7
Sandiway. L63 —5A 34
Sandiways Rd. L45 —5C 2
Sandlea Pk. L48 —5C 14
Sandon Cres. L64 —2C 42
Sandon Ind. Est. L5 —5D 4
Sandon Promenade. L44
—1A 12
Sandon Rd. L44 —1A 12
Sandon St. L8 —6H 13
Sandon Way. L5 —5D 4
Sandpiper Clo. L49 —1D 16
Sandridge Av. L45 —4F 3
Sandridge Rd. L61 —4B 24
Sandringham Av. L47 —5E 7
Sandringham Clo. L62 —2G 27
Sandringham Dri. L45 —3E 3
Sandringham Gdns. L65
—5B 48
Sandrock Rd. L45 —4F 3
Sands of Dee. L64 —3F 37
Sandstone. L45 —6G 3
Sandstone Dri. L48 —5G 15
Sandstone Wlk. L60 —4C 30
Sandy La. L45 —5C 2
Sandy La. L48 —6D 14
Sandy La. L60 —2C 30
Sandy La. L61 —2G 23
Sandy La. L64 —6E 37
Sandy La. N. L61 —2C 23
Sandymount Dri. L45 —4E 3
Sandymount Dri. L63 —4A 32
Sandy Way. L43 —2E 19
Sankey St. L1 —5G 13
Sarah St. L6 —1H 13
Saughall Massie La. L49
—2E 17
Saughall Massie Rd. L48
—4F 15
Saughall Massie Rd. L49
—1C 16
Saughall Rd. L46 —6C 8
Saxon Rd. L46 —4F 9
Saxon Rd. L47 —5E 7

Saxon Way. L66 —6A 46
Scafell Clo. L62 —2F 39
School Av. L64 —1D 42
School Clo. L46 —3F 9
Schoolfield Clo. L49 —5H 17
Schoolfield Rd. L49 —5H 17
School Hill. L60 —4B 30
School La. L43 —4A 10
School La. L44 —1C 10
School La. L47 —4F 7
(Great Meols)
School La. L47 —5D 6
(Hoylake, in two parts)
School La. L61 —3F 23
School La. L62 —2F 33
School La. L63 —3D 26
School La. L64 —1D 42
(Little Neston)
School La. L64 —3F 37
(Neston)
School La. L64 —4A 36
(Parkgate)
School Rd. L46 —4H 39
School Rd. L65 —2H 47
Schubert Clo. L66 —3E 47
Scoresby Rd. L46 —2H 9
Scotia Av. L62 —2A 28
Scotland Rd. L3 & L5 —2F 13
Scots Pl. L41 —6D 10
Scott Clo. L4 —4H 5
Scotton Av. L66 —2B 46
Scotts Quays. L41 —4A 12
Scott St. L45 —4F 3
Scythes, The. L49 —3C 16
Scythia Clo. L62 —2A 28
Seabank Av. L44 —6G 3
Seabank Cotts. L47 —3G 7
Seabank Rd. L41 —3B 20
Seabank Rd. L45 & L44 —3F 3
Seabank Rd. L66 —5A 30
Sea Brow. L1 —4E 13
Seacombe Dri. L66 —4E 47
Seacombe Promenade. L44
—1A 12
Seacombe Tower. L5 —5G 5
Seacombe View. L44 —3A 12
Sea Ct. Flats. L45 —4D 2
Seafield Av. L60 —5A 30
Seafield Rd. L45 —4E 3
Seafield Rd. L62 —1H 27
Seaforth Dri. L46 —6E 9
Sealy Clo. L63 —2G 33
Sea Rd. L45 —3D 2
Seaton Rd. L42 —3H 19
Seaton Rd. L45 —5E 3
Sea View. L47 —6D 6
Sea View. L64 —3C 42
Seaview Av. L45 —6E 3
Seaview Av. L61 —3H 23
Seaview Av. L62 —5F 35
Seaview La. L61 —3H 23
Seaview Rd. L45 —5E 3
Seawood Gro. L46 —6D 8
Second Av. L43 —1H 17
Sedbergh Rd. L44 —6D 2
Seddon St. L1 —5F 13
Sedgefield Clo. L46 —5G 9
Sedgefield Rd. L46 —5G 9
Seeley Av. L41 —6E 11
Seel St. L1 —4F 13
Sefton Clo. L45 —4C 20
Sefton Dri. L45 —4F 3
Sefton Rd. L62 —1G 27
Sefton St. L8 —1F 21
Selborne Clo. L66 —6H 13
Selborne St. L8 —6H 13
Selbourne Clo. L49 —4H 17
Selby Grn. L66 —2B 46
Selby St. L45 —6F 3
Selina Rd. L4 —1G 5
Selkirk Av. L62 —1G 39
Selkirk Clo. L66 —2H 45
Sellar St. L4 —4G 5
Selston Clo. L63 —1G 33
Selwyn St. L4 —2G 5
Serpentine Rd. L44 —6G 3

Servite Clo. L65 —1F 47
Servite Pl. L64 —6C 36
Sessions Rd. L4 —3G 5
Seven Acres La. L61 —3C 24
Seven Row. L64 —2C 42
Severn St. L5 —5H 5
Severn St. L41 —4E 11
Severnvale. L65 —4H 47
Seymour Ct. L42 —3A 20
Seymour Dri. L66 —1E 47
Seymour Pl. E. L45 —3G 3
Seymour Pl. W. L45 —3F 3
Seymour St. L3 —3G 13
Seymour St. L20 —1D 4
Seymour St. L42 —3A 20
Seymour St. L45 —3F 3
Shackleton Rd. L46 —1H 9
Shadwell St. L5 —6D 4
Shaftesbury St. L8 —1G 21
Shakespeare Av. L42 —6B 20
Shakespeare Rd. L44 —3H 11
Shakespeare Rd. L64 —4C 36
Shalam Ct. L63 —3D 26
Shalford Gro. L48 —5F 15
Shallmarsh Clo. L63 —4D 26
Shallmarsh Ct. L63 —4D 26
Shallmarsh Rd. L63 —4D 26
Shamrock Rd. L41 —6D 10
Sharpeville Clo. L4 —4F 5
Shavington Av. L43 —4D 18
Shawbury Av. L63 —2D 26
Shaw Clo. L66 —3F 47
Shaw Hill St. L1 —3F 13
Shaw La. L49 —5C 16
Shaws All. L1 —5E 13
Shaws Dri. L47 —4F 7
Shaw St. L6 —1H 13
Shaw St. L41 —2H 19
Shaw St. L47 —6D 6
Shearman Clo. L61 —5C 24
Shearman Rd. L61 —5C 24
Sheehan Heights. L5 —5E 5
Sheen Rd. L45 —5G 3
Sheepfield Clo. L66 —6C 40
Sheldon Clo. L63 —2G 33
Sheldrake Gro. L64 —2C 42
Shelley Way. L48 —1A 22
Shellway Rd. L65 —4D 48
Shelton Rd. L45 —5E 3
Shenley Clo. L63 —3F 27
Shepherd Clo. L49 —3C 16
Shepherd St. L6 —3H 13
Shepside Clo. L66 —5C 46
Shepston Av. L4 —2H 5
Shepton Rd. L66 —5E 47
Sherborne Rd. L44 —6D 2
Sherbourne Rd. L65 —4B 48
Sheridan St. L5 —1G 13
Sheriff Clo. L5 —1G 13
Sheringham Clo. L49 —6G 9
Sherlock La. L44 —3E 11
Sherlock St. L5 —4H 5
Sherry La. L49 —5G 17
Sherwood Av. L61 —3G 23
Sherwood Dri. L63 —2E 27
Sherwood Gro. L47 —5H 7
Sherwood Rd. L44 —2G 11
Sherwood Rd. L47 —5H 7
Sherwood St. L3 —6D 4
Shetland Dri. L62 —3C 34
Shetland Dri. L65 —6A 48
Shewell Clo. L42 —3H 19
Shiel Rd. L45 —4F 3
Shipton Clo. L43 —6C 18
Shirley St. L44 —2A 12
Shones Croft. L64 —2E 43
Shore Bank. L62 —1A 28
Shore Dri. L62 —3A 28
Shorefields. L62 —1A 28
Shorefields Village. L8 —4H 21
Shore La. L48 —2A 22
Shore Rd. L41 —6A 12
Shore Rd. L48 —2A 22
Shortfield Rd. L49 —3G 17
Shortfield Way. L49 —3G 17
Shotwick Helsby By-Pass. L66 & CH2 —6A 46
Shrewsbury Clo. L43 —1D 18
Shrewsbury Dri. L49 —1G 17
Shrewsbury Rd. L43 —6D 10
Shrewsbury Rd. L44 —6D 2
Shrewsbury Rd. L48 —6C 14
Shrewsbury Rd. L60 —2C 30
Shrewsbury Rd. L65 —2A 48
Shropshire Rd. L65 —4D 48
Sidings, The. L42 —5B 20
Sidlaw Clo. L66 —1A 46
Sidney Av. L45 —3E 3
Sidney Clo. L64 —4D 36
Sidney Gdns. L42 —3A 20
Sidney Rd. L20 —1F 5
Sidney Rd. L42 —4A 20
Sidney Rd. L64 —4D 36
Sidney Ter. L42 —4A 20
Silkhouse La. L2 —3E 13
Silverbeech Rd. L44 —2G 11
Silver Birches. L66 —6A 46
Silverbirch Gdns. L44 —6C 2
Silverbirch Way. L66 —6A 46
Silverburn Av. L46 —4E 9
Silverdale Rd. L43 —3E 19
Silverdale Rd. L63 —2F 27
Silverlea Av. L45 —6E 3
Silverne Dri. L65 —5G 47
Silvester St. L5 —6E 5
Simonsbridge. L48 —3B 22
Simpson St. L1 —6F 13
Simpson St. L41 —1H 19
Sim St. L3 —2G 13
Singleton Av. L42 —4G 19
Singleton Rd. L65 —3F 47
Sir Howard St. L8 —5H 13
Sir Howard Way. L8 —5H 13
Sir Thomas St. L1 —3E 13
Sisters Way. L41 —1H 19
Skelthorne St. L3 —4F 13
Skiddaw Rd. L62 —1C 34
Skipton Dri. L66 —3C 46
Skirving Pl. L5 —5F 5
Skirving St. L5 —5F 5
Slaidburn St. L5 —6G 5
Slater Pl. L1 —5F 13
Slater St. L1 —5F 13
Slatey Rd. L43 —1F 19
Sleepers Hill. L4 —4H 5
Slessor Av. L48 —4F 15
Slingsby Dri. L49 —3G 17
Smallwood M. L60 —1A 30
Smeaton St. L4 —2G 5
(in two parts)
Smeaton St. S. L4 —2G 5
Smilie Av. L46 —4C 8
Smith Av. L41 —5F 11
Smithdown La. L7 —4H 13
Smith Pl. L5 —5F 5
Smith St. L5 —4F 5
Smithy Clo. L64 —3E 43
Smithy Ct. L66 —1C 46
Smithy Hey. L48 —5E 15
Smithy Hill. L63 —5A 32
Smithy La. L4 —1H 5
Smithy La. L64 —6C 38
Smithy La. L66 —1C 46
Snab La. L64 —3D 42
Snabwood Clo. L64 —2C 42
Snowden La. L5 —6E 5
Snowden Rd. L46 —5C 8
Snowden Rd. L65 —2A 48
Snowdon Clo. L66 —1A 46
Snowdon Rd. L42 —5H 19
Snowdrop Av. L41 —5D 10
Snowdrop St. L5 —4F 5
Soho Pl. L3 —2G 13
Soho Sq. L3 —2G 13
Soho St. L3 —2G 13
(in two parts)
Solly Av. L42 —5A 20
Solway St. L41 —4D 10
Somerset Rd. L45 —6C 2
Somerset Rd. L48 —4E 15
Somerset Rd. L61 —5A 24
Somerville Clo. L63 —5H 33
Somerville Clo. L64 —2C 42
Somerville Cres. L65 —3A 48
Somerville St. Clo. L5 —5G 5
Sorrel Clo. L43 —2B 18
South Bank. L43 —4F 19
Southbourne Rd. L45 —6B 2
S. Chester St. L8 —1H 21
Southcroft Rd. L45 —6B 2
Southdale Rd. L42 —5A 20
South Dri. L49 —2G 17
South Dri. L60 —4C 30
South Dri. L61 —4G 23
Southern Cres. L8 —2G 21
S. Ferry Quay. L3 —1F 21
Southfield Rd. L66 —1C 46
South Gro. L8 —3H 21
South Hey Rd. L61 —5H 23
S. Hill Gro. L43 —4F 19
S. Hill Rd. L8 —4H 21
S. Hill Rd. L41 —3G 19
S. Hill Rd. L43 —3G 19
S. Hunter St. L1 —5G 13
S. John St. L1 —4E 13
South Pde. L48 —5C 14
South Pde. L64 —5A 36
S. Park Ct. L44 —2A 12
S. Park Way. L20 —1F 5
S. Pier Rd. L65 —2H 41
Southport Rd. L20 —1G 5
Southridge Rd. L61 —4C 24
South Rd. L42 —5G 19
South Rd. L48 —6D 14
South Rd. L65 —2D 48
(Ellesmere Port)
South Rd. L65 —4A 48
(Wolverham)
S. Sefton Bus. Cen. L20 —1D 4
South View. L62 —4B 28
South Vs. L45 —4F 3
Southwell Pl. L8 —2G 21
Southwell St. L8 —2G 21
Southwick Rd. L42 —4A 20
S. Wirral Retail Pk. L62 —6B 28
Sparks La. L61 —3C 24
Sparling St. L1 —6F 13
Speedwell Clo. L60 —3E 31
Speedwell Dri. L60 —3E 31
Speedwell Rd. L41 —6D 10
Spellow La. L4 —3H 5
Spencer Av. L46 —4G 9
Spencer St. L6 —1H 13
Spenser Av. L42 —6B 20
Spenser Rd. L64 —4C 36
Spinney Dri. L66 —4D 46
Spinney, The. L48 —5G 15
Spinney, The. L49 —1G 17
Spinney, The. L60 —6E 31
Spinney, The. L63 —6H 27
Spinney, The. L64 —5A 36
Spital Heyes. L63 —6H 27
Spital Rd. L62 —6A 28
Spital Rd. L63 & L62 —6G 27
Sprainger St. L3 —1D 12
Spring Av. L66 —1C 46
Springcroft. L64 —4A 36
Springfield. L3 —2G 13
(in two parts)
Springfield Av. L48 —4G 15
Springfield Clo. L49 —5A 18
Springfield Sq. L4 —3H 5
Spring Gdns. L66 —1C 46
Springhill Av. L62 —5B 34
Spring St. L42 —4B 20
Spring Vale. L45 —4C 2
Springwood Way. L63 —1G 27
Spunhill Av. L66 —5C 46
Spurgeon Clo. L5 —6H 5
Spurstow Clo. L43 —4D 18
Stable Clo. L49 —3D 16
Stackfield, The. L48 —4H 15
Stadium Rd. L62 —6C 28
Stafford Gdns. L65 —2H 47
Stafford St. L3 —3G 13
Stakes, The. L46 —2E 9
Stamford St. L65 —2G 47
Stanbury Av. L63 —3G 27
Standard Pl. L42 —4B 20
Standish St. L3 —2E 13
Stanfield Av. L5 —6H 5
Stanfield Dri. L63 —6F 27
Stanford Av. L45 —4F 3
Stanhope Dri. L62 —2B 34
Stanhope St. L8 —1F 21
(in two parts)
Stanlaw Rd. L65 —3A 48
Stanley Av. L45 —5B 2
Stanley Av. L63 —2B 26
Stanley Clo. L4 —4F 5
Stanley Clo. L44 —3A 12
Stanley Ct. L42 —4B 20
Stanley La. L62 —1H 39
Stanley Precinct. L20 —1F 5
Stanley Rd. L20 & L5 —1E 5
Stanley Rd. L41 —4D 10
Stanley Rd. L47 —1C 14
Stanley Rd. L62 —1G 27
Stanley Rd. L63 —1G 27
Stanley Rd. L65 —2G 41
Stanley St. L1 —3E 13
Stanley St. L44 —3A 12
Stanley Ter. L45 —4F 3
Stanmore Pk. L49 —4B 16
Stanney Clo. L62 —2G 39
Stanney Clo. L64 —6C 36
Stanney La. L65 & CH2 —3H 47
Stanney Mill La. CH2 —6D 48
Stanney Mill Rd. CH2 —4D 48
Stanney Mill Rd. L65 —4D 48
Stanney Woods Av. L65 —6A 48
Stanton Clo. L64 —5D 36
Stanton Ct. L64 —5C 36
(off Stanton Clo.)
Stanton Rd. L63 —6E 27
Stapleford Ct. L66 —5F 41
Stapleton Av. L49 —3D 16
Starbeck Dri. L66 —1B 46
Star St. L8 —1G 21
Starworth Dri. L62 —2A 28
Statham Rd. L43 —5A 10
Station App. L46 —3E 9
Station App. L47 —5G 7
Station Av. L66 —6C 40
Station Clo. L64 —6D 36
Station Grn. L66 —6C 40
Station Rd. L41 —4D 10
Station Rd. L44 —1E 11
Station Rd. L47 —1D 14
Station Rd. L60 —5B 30
Station Rd. L61 & L63 —4F 25
(Storeton Brickfields)
Station Rd. L61 —5E 23
(Thurstaston)
Station Rd. L64 —5E 43
(Burton)
Station Rd. L64 —6C 36
(Neston)
Station Rd. L64 —5A 36
(Parkgate)
Station Rd. L65 —1A 48
(in two parts)
Station Rd. L66 —1C 46
Stavordale Rd. L46 —4F 9
Steble St. L8 —2H 21
Steel Av. L45 —5G 3
Steel Ct. L5 —5E 5
Steeple Ct. L64 —6C 36
Steeple, The. L48 —3B 22
Steers St. L6 —1H 13
Steinberg Ct. L3 —1E 13
Stephens Gdns. L66 —1B 46
Stephens La. L2 —3E 13
Stephens Ter. L66 —1B 46
Stepney Gro. L4 —2H 5
Sterling Way. L5 —5F 5
Stevenson Dri. L63 —6F 27
Stevens Rd. L60 —4E 31
Stewart Clo. L61 —6B 24
Stirling Ct. L65 —4B 48
Stirling St. L44 —3F 11
Stockbridge Pl. L5 —5H 5
Stockbridge St. L5 —6H 5
Stockdale Clo. L3 —2E 13
Stoddart Rd. L4 —1H 5
Stoke Clo. L62 —2G 39
Stoke Gdns. L65 —3A 48
Stokesay. L43 —1B 18
Stokesay Ct. L65 —4C 48
Stoke St. L41 —5F 11
Stoke Wlk. L65 —3A 48
Stonebank Dri. L64 —1E 43
Stoneby Dri. L45 —4E 3
Stonehey Dri. L48 —1A 22
Stonehill Av. L63 —3G 27
Stonehouse Rd. L44 —6C 2
Stoneleigh Gro. L42 —1F 27
Stoneridge Ct. L43 —5A 10
Stone St. L3 —1D 12
Stoney Hey Rd. L45 —4E 3
Stonham Clo. L49 —2E 17
Stopford St. L8 —3H 21
Store St. L20 —2F 5
Storeton Clo. L43 —4E 19
Storeton La. L61 —6E 25
Storeton Rd. L43 & L42 —4F 19
Stourcliffe Rd. L44 —1E 11
Stour Ct. L65 —6H 41
Stourport Clo. L49 —3C 16
Stourton St. L44 —3G 11
Stowell St. L7 —5H 13
Strada Way. L3 —2H 13
Straker Av. L65 —1F 47
Strand Rd. L47 —5D 6
Strand St. L1 —4E 13
Strand, The. L2 —4D 12
Stratford Rd. L64 —1C 42
Strathallan Clo. L60 —1A 30
Strathcona Rd. L45 —5F 3
Strathearn Rd. L60 —4B 30
Strawberry Dri. L66 —6B 46
Strawberry Grn. L66 —6B 46
Street Hey La. L64 —2D 38
Stretton Av. L44 —1E 11
Stretton Clo. L43 —4C 18
Stretton Clo. L62 —2G 39
Stringhey Rd. L44 —6G 3
Stroud Clo. L49 —4C 16
Stuart Av. L46 —4F 9
Stuart Clo. L46 —5G 9
Stuart Gro. L20 —2F 5
Stuart Rd. L42 —4H 19
Studholme St. L20 —4E 5
Studley Rd. L45 —5C 2
Sudworth Rd. L45 —4E 3
Suffield Rd. L4 —3F 5
Suffolk Av. L65 —2F 47
Suffolk St. L1 —5F 13
Sugnall St. L7 —5H 13
(in two parts)
Sullivan Av. L49 —3F 17
Summerfield. L62 —1B 34
Summer Seat. L3 —1F 13
Summers Rd. L3 —2F 21
Summertrees Av. L49 —3D 16
Summertrees Clo. L49 —3D 16
Summertrees Rd. L66 —5E 47
Summerwood. L61 —2H 23
Summit, The. L44 —6G 3
Sumner Clo. L5 —6E 5
Sumner Rd. L41 —5D 10
Sumner Rd. L43 —5D 10
Sunbury Rd. L44 —2G 11
Suncroft Rd. L60 —4E 31
Sundridge St. L8 —3H 21
Sunfield Clo. L66 —4D 46
Sunfield Rd. L46 —3F 9
Sunningdale. L46 —5F 9
Sunningdale Dri. L61 —4C 24
Sunningdale Dri. L63 —5H 33
Sunningdale Rd. L45 —3D 2
Sunningdale Way. L64 —2C 42
Sunnybank. L49 —1F 17
Sunny Bank. L63 —3D 26
Sunnybank Av. L43 —3B 18
Sunnyside. L46 —3D 8
Sunnyside. L65 —1A 48
(off Church St.)
Surrey Av. L49 —2F 17
Surrey Dri. L48 —1A 22
Surrey St. L1 —5F 13
Surrey St. L44 —2E 11
Susan Gro. L46 —5D 8
Sussex Clo. L61 —5A 24
Sussex Rd. L48 —4E 15
Sutherland Dri. L62 —1F 39
Sutton Av. L64 —1C 42
Sutton Clo. L62 —2G 39
Sutton Hall Dri. L66 —1A 46
Sutton Hall Gdns. L66 —1A 46
Sutton Rd. L45 —4F 3
Sutton Way. L66 & L65 —3D 46
Swaledale Clo. L62 —6C 34
Swale Rd. L65 —6G 41
Swanston Av. L4 —2H 5
Sweetfield Gdns. L66 —6D 40
Sweetfield Rd. L66 —6D 40
Sweeting St. L2 —4E 13
Swift Weint. L64 —4A 36
Swindon Clo. L5 —4F 5
Swindon Clo. L49 —3C 16
Swindon St. L5 —4F 5
Sybil Rd. L4 —4H 5
Sycamore Av. L49 —6D 8
Sycamore Clo. L49 —6D 8
Sycamore Ct. L8 —3H 21
(off Weller Way)
Sycamore Dri. L66 —6F 47
Sycamore Rise. L49 —5C 16
Sycamore Rd. L42 —3H 19
Sylvandale Gro. L62 —1B 34
Syren St. L20 —2E 5
Sytchcroft. L64 —5C 36
Sytchcroft. L64 —5C 36

Tabley Clo. L43 —5D 18
Tabley St. L1 —5F 13
Talbot Av. L63 —2A 32
Talbot Av. L64 —1D 42
Talbot Clo. L64 —1D 42
Talbot Ct. L43 —3E 19
Talbot Gdns. L64 —1D 42
Talbot Rd. L43 —3E 19
Talbot Rd. L66 —4F 47
Taliesin St. L5 —6F 5
Tamworth Gro. L46 —4B 8
Tamworth St. L8 —2G 21
Tanar Clo. L62 —6H 27
Tanar Clo. L63 —6H 27
Tancred Rd. L4 —4H 5
Tancred Rd. L45 —6E 3
Tannery La. L64 —5C 36
Tansley Clo. L48 —5G 15
Tarbot Hey. L46 —5C 8
Target Rd. L60 —3G 29
Tariff St. L5 —6E 5
Tarleton St. L1 —4F 13
Tarporley Clo. L43 —4D 18
Tarporley Rd. L66 —3E 47
Tarran Dri. L46 —3D 8
Tarran Rd. L46 —3D 8
Tarran Way E. L46 —2D 8
Tarran Way Ind. Est. L46 —3D 8
Tarran Way N. L46 —2D 8
Tarran Way S. L46 —3D 8
Tarran Way W. L46 —2D 8
Tarvin Clo. L65 —3A 48
Tarvin Rd. L62 —1H 39
Tate St. L4 —3H 5
Tatlock St. L5 —1E 13
Tatlock Tower. L5 —6E 5
Tattersall Pl. L20 —1D 4
Tatton Rd. L42 —2H 19
Taunton Rd. L45 —5C 2
Tavener Clo. L63 —6A 34
Tavistock Rd. L45 —5D 2
Tavistock Wlk. L8 —3H 21
Tawd St. L4 —3G 5
Taylor St. L5 —6F 5
Taylor St. L41 —6A 12
Taylor St. Ind. Est. L5 —6F 5
(off Taylor St.)
Teals Way. L60 —3A 30
Tebay Rd. L62 —3C 34
Teehey Clo. L63 —3D 26
Teehey Gdns. L63 —3D 26
Teehey La. L63 —3D 26
Tees Clo. L4 —2F 5
Tees Ct. L65 —6G 41
Teesdale Rd. L63 —5E 27
Tees Pl. L4 —2G 5

62 A-Z Wirral

Tees St. L4 —2F 5
Tees St. L41 —4D 10
Teilo St. L8 —2H 21
Telegraph La. L45 —6A 2
Telegraph Rd. L48, L61 & L60
—2D 22
Telford Clo. L43 —3F 19
Telford Rd. L65 —3C 48
Telford's Quay. L65 —2H 41
Tempest Hey. L2 —3E 13
Temple Ct. L2 —4E 13
Temple La. L2 —3E 13
Templemore Rd. L43 —3E 19
Temple Rd. L42 —5G 19
Temple St. L2 —3E 13
Tenby Dri. L46 —5F 9
Tenby St. L5 —5H 5
Tennyson Av. L42 —6B 20
Tennyson Rd. L36 47
Tennyson Wlk. L8 —1H 21
Tenterden St. L1 —1F 13
Terminus Rd. L62 —6B 28
Tern Way. L46 —4B 8
Tetbury St. L41 —2G 19
Tetchill Clo. L66 —5D 46
Tetlow St. L4 —3H 5
Tetlow Way. L4 —3H 5
Teulon Clo. L4 —3G 5
Tewkesbury Clo. L66 —6A 46
Thackeray Pl. L8 —1H 21
Thackeray Sq. L8 —1H 21
Thackeray St. L8 —1H 21
Thamesdale. L65 —4H 47
Thames Gdns. L46 —5G 47
Thames Side. L65 —4H 47
Thelwall Rd. L66 —3E 47
Thermal Rd. L62 —5B 28
Thermopylae. L43 —1B 18
Thermopylae Pass. L43 —1A 18
(in two parts)
Thingwall Dri. L61 —3C 24
Thingwall Rd. L61 —3H 23
Thingwall Rd. E. L61 —3C 24
Third Av. L48 —1H 17
Thirlmere Av. L43 —1A 18
Thirlmere Dri. L45 —6F 3
Thirlmere Rd. L5 —6H 5
Thirlmere Rd. L64 —1C 42
Thirlmere Rd. L65 —5H 47
Thistledown Clo. L17 —4H 21
Thistleton Av. L41 —5D 10
Thomas Clo. L65 —5H 47
Thomas St. L41 —2A 20
(in two parts)
Thomaston St. L5 —5G 5
(in two parts)
Thomas Winder Ct. L5 —5F 5
Thompson St. L41 —3A 20
Thorburn Clo. L62 —1H 27
Thorburn Ct. L62 —6D 20
Thorburn Cres. L62 —1H 27
Thorburn Rd. L62 —1H 27
Thorncliffe Rd. L44 —2E 11
Thorncroft Dri. L61 —5D 24
Thorndale St. L5 —4G 5
Thorne Dri. L66 —2B 46
Thorne La. L44 —6D 2
Thorness Clo. L49 —5C 16
Thorneycroft St. L41 —5E 11
Thornfield Hey. L63 —1G 33
Thornham Clo. L49 —6G 9
Thornleigh Av. L62 —1H 39
Thornleigh Dri. L66 —1E 47
Thornley Rd. L46 —6B 8
Thornridge. L46 —5G 9
Thorns Dri. L49 —5C 16
Thornton Av. L63 —1D 26
Thornton Comn. L63
—5A 32
Thornton Cres. L60 —5D 30
Thornton Gro. L63 —1D 26
Thornton M. L66 —5D 46
Thornton Pl. L18 —3H 21
Thornton Rd. L45 —5E 3
Thornton Rd. L63 & L42
—1D 26
Thornton Rd. L65 —3B 48

Thornton St. L41 —5E 11
Thorntree Clo. L17 —4H 21
Thornwythe Gro. L66 —3E 47
Thorpe Bank. L42 —1F 27
Thorstone Dri. L61 —2G 23
Thorsway. L42 —5B 20
Thorsway. L48 —1B 22
Thresher Av. L49 —3C 16
Thursby Rd. L62 —1C 34
Thurstaston Rd. L60 —2A 30
Thurstaston Rd. L61 —4F 23
Tichbourne Way. L6 —2H 13
Tide Way. L45 —3C 2
Tillotson Clo. L8 —2G 21
Tilstock Av. L62 —1H 27
Tilstock Cres. L43 —6D 18
Tilston Rd. L45 —5E 3
Tinas Way. L49 —2G 17
Tinsley St. L4 —4H 5
Tintern Dri. L46 —5E 9
Titchfield St. L5 & L3 —1E 13
Tithebarn Clo. L60 —4B 30
Tithebarn Dri. L61 —5D 24
Tithebarn St. L2 —3E 13
Tiverton Av. L44 —1E 11
Tobin Clo. L5 —1E 13
Tobin St. L44 —1H 11
Toleman Av. L63 —4G 27
Tollemache Rd. L41 & L43
—6C 10
Tollemache St. L45 —3G 3
Tolpuddle Way. L4 —3F 5
Tom Mann Clo. L3 —2E 13
Topgate Clo. L60 —3D 30
Torcross St. L44 —2A 12
Torridon Gro. L66 —4F 47
Torrington Dri. L61 —3D 24
Torrington Gdns. L61 —2D 24
Torrington Rd. L44 —1E 11
Torr St. L5 —5G 5
(in two parts)
Torwood. L43 —1B 18
Tower Gdns. L3 —4D 12
Tower Hill. L42 —4H 19
Tower Promenade. L45 —2G 3
Tower Quays. L41 —5A 12
Tower Rd. L41 —5A 12
Tower Rd. L42 —6F 19
(Prenton)
Tower Rd. L42 —4H 19
(Tranmere)
Tower Rd. N. L60 —1A 30
Tower Rd. S. L60 —2B 30
Towers, The. L42 —5A 20
Tower St. L3 —2F 21
Tower Wharf. L41 —5A 12
Townfield Clo. L43 —4C 18
Townfield Gdns. L63 —2F 27
Townfield La. L43 —4C 18
Townfield La. L63 —2F 27
Townfield Rd. L48 —5D 14
Town Fields. L45 —5C 2
Townfield Way. L44 —1F 11
Town La. L63 —3E 27
Town La. L64 —1D 42
Town Meadow La. L46 —4B 8
Town Rd. L42 —4H 19
Townsend La. L5 —5D 4
Townsend St. L41 —4D 10
Townshend Av. L61 —4H 23
Towson St. L5 —5H 5
(in two parts)
Toxteth Gro. L8 —3H 21
Toxteth St. L8 —2H 21
Trafalgar Av. L44 —6H 3
Trafalgar Dri. L63 —5G 27
Trafalgar Rd. L44 —6G 3
Trafalgar Way. L6 —2H 13
Treborth St. L8 —2H 21
Treetops. L64 —2C 42
Treforris Rd. L45 —4D 2
Trentdale. L65 —4H 47
Trentham Rd. L44 —2G 11
Trent St. L5 —5E 5
Trent St. L41 —4D 10
Trent Way. L60 —5E 31
Trevelyan St. L9 —1H 5

Trimley Clo. L49 —2E 17
Trinity Ct. L47 —6D 6
Trinity La. L41 —4A 12
Trinity Pl. L20 —1F 5
Trinity Rd. L20 —1E 5
Trinity Rd. L44 —6F 3
Trinity Rd. L47 —5D 6
Trinity St. L41 —6G 11
Trinity Wlk. L3 —2G 13
Troon Clo. L63 —6A 34
Troutbeck Clo. L49 —5G 17
Trowbridge St. L3 —4G 13
Trueman Clo. L43 —5A 10
Trueman St. L3 —3F 13
Trumans La. L66 —6C 40
Tudor Av. L44 —3A 12
Tudor Av. L63 —6G 27
Tudor Clo. L7 —4H 13
Tudor Clo. L66 —6A 46
Tudor Grange. L49 —4D 16
Tudor Rd. L42 —4A 20
Tudorville Rd. L63 —4F 27
Tudorway. L60 —3D 30
Tulip Av. L41 —5D 10
Tunstall Clo. L49 —2E 17
Tupman St. L8 —2H 21
Turmar Av. L61 —3D 24
Turnberry Clo. L46 —4B 8
Turner St. L41 —2G 19
Turney Rd. L44 —1E 11
Turret Rd. L45 —5E 3
Turriff Dri. L63 —1E 39
Turrocks Clo. L64 —2C 42
Turrocks Croft. L64 —2C 42
Turton St. L5 —5F 5
Tweed St. L41 —4E 11
Twickenham Dri. L46 —2F 9
Twiss St. L8 —2H 21
Two Acre Gro. L66 —6F 47
Twomey Clo. L5 —1E 13
Tyburn Clo. L63 —1F 33
Tyburn Rd. L63 —1F 33
Tyne Clo. L4 —3G 5
Tynemouth Clo. L5 —6H 5
Tynesdale. L65 —4H 47
Tyne St. L41 —4D 10
Tynron Gro. L43 —3B 18
Tynwald Rd. L48 —5C 14
Tyrer St. L1 —4F 13
Tyrer St. L41 —4D 10

U
Ullapool Clo. L66 —1H 45
Ullswater Av. L43 —1B 18
Ullswater Rd. L65 —5A 48
Ulverscroft. L43 —3D 18
Underley Ter. L62 —2H 27
Underwood Dri. L65 —5H 47
Union St. L2 —4E 13
Union St. L3 —3D 12
Union St. L41 —4B 20
Union St. L44 —1H 11
Union Ter. L45 —2F 3
Upavon Rd. L49 —4B 16
Upland Rd. L49 —1F 17
Uplands Rd. L62 —2A 34
Up. Beau St. L5 —1G 13
Up. Beckwith St. L41 —5F 11
Up. Brassey St. L41 —5D 10
Up. Bute St. L5 —1G 13
Up. Canning St. L8 —5H 13
Up. Duke St. L1 —5G 13
Up. Essex St. L8 —2H 21
Up. Flaybrick Rd. L41 —6C 10
Up. Frederick St. L1 —5F 13
(in two parts)
Up. Hampton St. L8 —6H 13
Up. Harrington St. L8 —1G 21
Up. Hill St. L8 —1G 21
(in three parts)
Up. Hope Pl. L7 —5H 13
Up. Huskisson St. L8 —6H 13
Up. Mann St. L8 —1G 21
Up. Mersey St. L65 —2G 41
Up. Newington. L1 —4G 13
Up. Park St. L8 —2H 21
Up. Parliament St. L8 —6G 13

Up. Pitt St. L1 —5F 13
Up. Pownall St. L1 —5F 13
Up. Raby Rd. L64 —6H 43
Up. Rice La. L44 —6G 3
Up. Stanhope St. L8 —6G 13
Upton By-Pass. L49 —3F 17
Upton Clo. L49 —2F 17
Upton Ct. L49 —1F 17
Upton Pk. Dri. L49 —1G 17
Upton Rd. L41 & L41 —2A 18
Upton Rd. L46 —5E 9
Upton Rd. L66 —3D 46
Ure Ct. L65 —6G 41
Urmson Rd. L45 —6F 3
Ursula St. L20 —1F 5
Utkinton Clo. L43 —4D 18
UVECO Bus. Cen. L41 —4F 11

V
Vale Dri. L45 —4G 3
Vale Gdns. L65 —3H 47
Valentia Rd. L47 —1C 14
Valerian Rd. L41 —6D 10
Vale Rd. L65 —3H 47
Valkyrie Rd. L45 —3C 2
Valleybrook Gro. L63 —1H 33
Valley Dri. L66 —1D 46
Valley Rd. L41 —4C 10
Valley Rd. L62 —3B 34
Valley View. L66 —2D 46
Vanderbyl Av. L62 —1A 34
Vandries St. L3 —1D 12
Vanguard St. L5 —4H 5
Vardon St. L41 —5G 11
Varthen St. L5 —4H 5
Vaughan Rd. L45 —4F 3
Vaughan St. L41 —5D 10
Vauxhall Rd. L3 & L5 —2E 13
Venables Clo. L63 —2H 33
Venables Dri. L63 —1G 33
Venice St. L5 —5H 5
Venmore St. L5 —5H 5
Vere St. L8 —2G 21
(in two parts)
Vernon Av. L44 —3H 11
Vernon Av. L66 —2H 27
Vernon St. L2 —3E 13
Verona St. L5 —5H 5
Veronica Way. L66 —6D 40
Verulam Clo. L8 —6H 13
Verwood Clo. L61 —2H 23
Vescock St. L5 —6F 5
Vesuvius Pl. L5 —5F 5
Vesuvius St. L5 —5F 5
Vicarage Clo. L42 —6F 19
Vicarage Gro. L44 —6G 3
Vicarage La. L64 —5H 43
Viceroy St. L5 —5H 5
Vickers St. L8 —2H 21
Victoria Av. L60 —5C 30
Victoria Dri. L42 —6G 20
Victoria Dri. L48 —5C 14
Victoria Gdns. L43 —3F 19
Victoria La. L43 —3F 19
Victoria Mt. L43 —3F 19
Victoria Pde. L45 —2G 3
Victoria Pk. Rd. L42 —5H 19
Victoria Pl. L44 —3A 12
Victoria Rd. L42 —3G 19
Victoria Rd. L45 —3E 3
(in two parts)
Victoria Rd. L48 —6D 14
Victoria Rd. L63 —3D 26
Victoria Rd. L64 —1D 42
Victoria Rd. L65 —2H 41
Victoria St. L2 & L1 —4E 13
Victoria St. L42 —4H 27
Vienna St. L5 —5H 5
Village Clo. L45 —2G 3
Village Grn. Ct. L43 —5A 10
Village Rd. L43 —3E 19
Village Rd. L48 —5E 15
Village Rd. L60 —4B 30
Village Rd. L63 —3D 26

Village St. L6 —1H 13
Village, The. L63 —4G 27
Village, The. L64 —6H 43
Village Way. L45 —5C 2
Vincent Ct. L1 —5F 13
Vincent St. L41 —2H 19
Vine Rd. L66 —6F 47
Vine St. L7 —5H 13
Vine St. L41 —6G 11
Vining St. L8 —1H 21
Viola St. L20 —2E 5
Violet Rd. L41 —6D 10
Virgil St. L5 —1F 13
Virginia Rd. L45 —2F 3
Virginia St. L3 —3D 12
Virginia Ter. L66 —5B 40
Vittoria Clo. L41 —6H 11
Vittoria St. L41 —6H 11
Vittoria St. L41 —6H 11
Vivian Av. L44 —3A 12
Vulcan Clo. L41 —5D 10
Vulcan St. L3 —1D 12
Vulcan St. L41 —6D 10
Vyner Clo. L43 —1C 18
Vyner Ct. L43 —1C 18
Vyner Rd. L45 —6D 2
Vyner Rd. N. L43 —6B 10
Vyner Rd. S. L43 —1B 18
Vyrnwy St. L5 —4H 5

W
Wadham Pk. L20 —1F 5
Wadham Rd. L20 —2E 5
Wakefield Dri. L46 —1F 9
Wakefield Rd. L66 —6D 46
Wakefield St. L3 —2G 13
Walby Clo. L49 —5A 18
Walden Dri. L66 —6F 45
Waldron Clo. L3 —2E 13
Walford Clo. L63 —1F 33
Walker M. L42 —4H 19
Walker Pl. L42 —4H 19
Walker's Croft. L45 —6D 2
Walkers La. L66 —1C 46
Walker St. L42 —4H 19
Walker St. L47 —6D 6
Walker St. L62 —3H 27
Wallacre Rd. L44 —1C 10
Wallasey Bri. Rd. L41 —4D 10
Wallasey Rd. L44 & L45
—1D 10
Wallasey Village. L45 & L44
—5C 2
Wallcroft. L64 —6C 38
Waller Clo. L4 —4G 5
Wallingford Rd. L49 —3F 17
Wallrake. L60 —4B 30
Walmsley St. L5 —5E 5
Walmsley St. L44 —6G 3
Walnut Gro. L66 —6F 47
Walnut St. L7 —4H 13
Walsh Clo. L5 —1E 13
Walsingham Rd. L44 —2H 11
Walter St. L5 —6D 4
Walton Breck Rd. L4 —4H 5
Walton La. L4 —4H 5
Walton Pk. Gdns. L4 —1H 5
Walton Rd. L4 —4G 5
Walton St. L41 —1A 20
Walton Village. L4 —1H 5
Wapping. L1 —5F 13
Wapping Quay. L3 —6E 13
Warden St. L4 —4G 5
Ward Gro. L42 —1F 27
Ward St. L3 —3G 13
Waring Av. L42 —5H 19
Warkworth Clo. L65 —4C 48
Warren Ct. L66 —4D 46
Warren Dri. L43 —1A 18
Warren Dri. L45 —3D 2
Warren Dri. L66 —6E 41
Warren Hey. L63 —2G 33
Warren Hurst. L45 —3E 3
Warren, The. L49 —2H 17
Warren Way. L60 —2H 29

Warrington Av. L65 —5H 47
Warrington St. L41 —3A 20
Warwick Clo. L43 —2G 19
Warwick Clo. L64 —2C 42
Warwick Ct. L8 —1H 21
Warwick Rd. L65 —5C 48
Warwick Dri. L45 —5G 3
Warwick Rd. L48 —1A 22
Warwick Rd. L49 —2E 17
Warwick St. L8 —1G 21
Washbrook Av. L43 —4A 10
Wastdale Av. L46 —4C 8
Wastdale Dri. L46 —4C 8
Wastdale M. L46 —4C 8
Waterfield Clo. L63 —4D 26
Waterford Dri. L64 —6E 37
Waterford Rd. L43 —2D 18
Waterhouse St. L5 —1H 13
Waterloo Clo. L65 —2A 48
Waterloo Ct. L63 —3G 27
Waterloo Pl. L41 —2A 20
Waterloo Quay. L3 —2D 12
Waterloo Rd. L3 —1D 12
Waterloo Rd. L45 —2F 3
Waterpark Clo. L43 —6E 19
Waterpark Rd. L43 & L42
—6D 18
Water St. L3 & L2 —4D 12
Water St. L41 —1B 20
Water St. L44 —1H 11
Water St. L45 —4A 28
Water Tower Rd. L64 —4C 36
Waterworks La. L66 —4G 39
Watkinson St. L1 —6F 13
Watmough St. L5 —1G 13
Watson St. L41 —6H 11
Waverley Gro. L42 —5G 19
Waverley Rd. L47 —6E 7
Waverton Av. L43 —5C 18
Waverton Rd. L66 —2E 47
Wavertree Ct. L66 —6F 41
Weald Dri. L66 —1A 46
Weatherby. L49 —3H 17
Weaver Rd. L65 —4A 48
Weaver St. L9 —1H 5
Webster Av. L44 —6H 3
Websters La. L66 —5F 47
Webster St. L3 —3F 13
Weldon St. L4 —1H 5
Welford Av. L43 —5D 18
Welland Rd. L63 —4D 26
Wellbrae Clo. L49 —2D 16
Weller Way. L8 —2H 21
Wellesbourne Clo. L64 —1B 42
Wellesley Av. L65 —2A 48
Wellesley Rd. L44 —1F 11
Wellesley Wlk. L65 —2A 48
Wellington Clo. L63 —3G 27
Wellington Clo. L65 —2A 48
Wellington Rd. L8 —3H 21
Wellington Rd. L43 —2E 19
Wellington Rd. L45 —2E 3
Wellington Rd. L63 —3G 27
(in two parts)
Wellington Rd. N. L65 —2A 48
Wellington St. L3 —1F 13
Wellington Ter. L8 —2H 21
Wellington Ter. L41 —2H 19
Well La. L42 —4H 19
Well La. L49 —4C 16
Well La. L60 —5C 30
Well La. L63 —3D 26
Well La. L66 —2C 47
Wells Clo. L66 —6A 46
Wellswood Rd. L66 —6E 41
Welshampton Clo. L66 —5D 46
Welsh Rd. L66 —6F 45
Welton Av. L49 —2F 17
Welton Rd. L62 —1C 34
Wendover Clo. L43 —3B 18
Wenlock Gdns. L66 —5F 47
Wenlock La. L66 —5F 47
Wensleydale Av. L62 —6C 34

Wentworth Av. L45 —4F 3
Wentworth Clo. L43 —3B 18
Wentworth Dri. L5 —1H 13
Wentworth Dri. L63 —6H 33
Wernbrook Clo. L43 —3B 18
Wervin Clo. L43 —5C 18
Wervin Rd. L43 —5C 18
Wesley Av. L44 —6G 3
Wesley Clo. L64 —5B 36
Wesley Gro. L44 —2A 12
Westbank Av. L45 —4G 3
Westbank Rd. L42 —4G 19
Westbourne Av. L48 —5D 14
Westbourne Gro. L48 —5D 14
Westbourne Rd. L43 & L41
　—2G 19
Westbourne Rd. L44 —1D 10
Westbourne Rd. L48 —5D 14
Westbourne St. L6 —2H 13
(in two parts)
Westbourne Wlk. L6 —2H 13
Westbrook Rd. L46 —6C 8
Westbury St. L41 —3A 20
West Clo. L43 —2B 18
Westdale Rd. L42 —5A 20
W. Derby Rd. L6 —2H 13
W. Derby St. L7 —3H 13
West Dri. L49 —3A 20
West Dri. L60 —4C 30
West Dri. L64 —1B 42
Westenra Av. L65 —6F 41
Western Av. L62 —5B 28
Westfield Rd. L44 —4H 11
Westgate Rd. L62 —5H 27
West Gro. L60 —3B 30
Westhouse Clo. L63 —6A 34
W. Kirby Concourse. L48
　—5C 14
W. Kirby Rd. L48 & L46 —2B 16
W. Knowe. L43 —3E 19
Westlands Clo. L44 —4H 1
Westminster Bri. L65 —2A 48
Westminster Clo. L4 —2G 5
Westminster Ct. L42 —4B 34
Westminster Dri. L62 —4B 34
Westminster Gro. L65 —1A 48
Westminster Ind. Est. L65
　—1F 47
Westminster Rd. L4 —2F 5
Westminster Rd. L44 —1F 11
Westminster Rd. L65 —1A 48
Westmoreland Pl. L5 —6F 5
Westmoreland Rd. L45 —4G 3
West Pk. Dri. L66 —6A 46
W. Park Gdns. L43 —5A 10
West Rd. L43 —2B 18
West Rd. L62 —2C 40
West Rd. L65 —4A 48
W. Rumney Rd. L4 —3F 5
West St. L45 —6F 3
West Vale. L64 —1C 42
West View. L41 —3B 20
West View. L45 —3E 3
West View. L66 —5A 40
Westview Clo. L43 —3B 18
Westward Ho. L48 —3B 22
Westward View. L17 —4H 21
West Way. L43 —3B 18
West Way. L46 —4E 9
Westway. L49 —3E 17
Westway. L60 —5B 30

W. Way Sq. L46 —4E 9
Westwood Ct. L64 —3C 36
Westwood Gro. L44 —1E 11
Westwood Rd. L43 —1A 18
Wetherby Av. L45 —4F 3
Wetherby Way. L66 —1B 46
Wethersfield Rd. L43 —4C 18
Wetstone La. L48 —6E 15
Wexford Clo. L43 —3C 18
Wexford Rd. L43 —3D 18
Weybourne Clo. L49 —6G 9
Weymoor Clo. L63 —1F 33
Whaley La. L61 —3B 24
Whalley Rd. L42 —2H 19
Whalley St. L8 —3H 21
Whardale Dri. L62 —6D 34
Wharfedale Av. L42 —5F 19
Wharfedale Rd. L45 —5D 2
Wharfe La. L65 —6G 41
Wharf Rd. L41 —4D 10
Wharf St. L62 —4H 27
Wharton Clo. L49 —1D 16
Wheatfield Clo. L46 —6F 9
Wheatfields Clo. L66 —5C 46
Wheatland Bus. Pk. L44 —3H 11
Wheatland La. L44 —2H 11
Wheatland Rd. L60 —4E 31
Wheldrake Clo. L66 —2B 46
Wheatstone Hey. L66 —2D 46
Whetstone La. L41 —2H 19
Whinmoor Clo. L43 —1B 18
Whitby Av. L45 —6C 2
Whitby La. CH1 —6B 46
Whitby Rd. L65 —3H 47
Whitebeam Av. L66 —6F 47
Whitebeam Wlk. L49 —5B 16
Whitechapel. L1 —4F 13
Whitecroft Rd. L66 —5E 47
Whitefield Av. L4 —3G 5
Whitefield Way. L6 —1H 13
Whitegates Clo. L64 —4A 38
Whitegates Cres. L64 —5A 38
Whitehall Clo. L4 —2G 5
Whitehaven Way. L46 —2F 9
Whitehouse La. L60 & L63
　—2E 31
Whitelands Meadow. L49
　—2E 17
White Lodge Clo. L62 —6B 34
Whitemere Ct. L65 —2G 41
Whiteside Clo. L5 —6F 5
Whiteside Clo. L49 —3G 17
White St. L1 —5F 13
Whitewell Dri. L49 —1F 17
Whitfield Ct. L42 —3H 19
Whitfield La. L60 —2C 30
Whitfield St. L42 —3H 19
Whitford Rd. L42 —3G 19
Whitley Dri. L44 —6H 3
Whitley St. L3 —1D 12
Whittle Clo. L5 —5G 5
Whittle St. L5 —4G 5
Wickham Clo. L44 —3H 11
Wicklow Clo. L66 —1A 46
Widgeons Covert. L63 —6H 31
Wiend, The. L42 —6H 19
Wiend, The. L63 —4G 27
Wight Clo. L65 —6B 48
Wilbraham Pl. L5 —6F 5
Wilbraham St. L5 —6F 5
Wilbraham St. L41 —1A 20

Wilburn St. L4 —2H 5
Wilde St. L3 —3G 13
Wilkes Av. L46 —2H 9
Wilkinson St. L65 —1H 47
Wilkinson St. N. L65 —1A 48
Wilkin St. L4 —4G 5
Willan St. L43 —3F 19
Willaston Grn. M. L64 —5B 38
Willaston Rd. L46 —4D 8
Willaston Rd. L63 —3H 37
William Brown St. L1 —3F 13
William Brown St. L3 —3F 13
William Henry St. L3 —2G 13
William Henry St. L20 —1D 4
William Johnson Gdns. L65
　—1A 48
William Moult St. L5 —6F 5
Williamson Sq. L1 —4F 13
Williamson St. L1 —4F 13
William St. L41 —1A 20
William St. L44 —3A 12
Willington Av. L62 —2G 39
Willmer Rd. L42 —2G 19
Willoughby Rd. L44 —1D 10
Willowbank Rd. L42 —4H 19
Willowbank Rd. L62 —3H 27
Willowbrow. L63 —1F 37
Willowcroft Rd. L44 —3G 11
Willowdale Way. L66 —6F 47
Willow Gro. L46 —6D 8
Willow Gro. L66 —6B 46
Willow La. L63 —2H 37
Willow Lea. L43 —3E 19
Willow Pk. L49 —3C 16
Willows, The. L45 —4C 2
Wilmslow Av. L66 —2E 47
Wilmslow Dri. L66 —3E 47
Wilne Rd. L45 —5E 3
Wilson Av. L44 —1A 12
Wilson Rd. L44 —1A 12
Wilson La. L65 —4G 47
Wilson St. L8 —3H 21
Wilson Wlk. L8 —3H 21
Wilstan Av. L63 —4D 26
Wilton Grange. L48 —3C 14
Wilton Rd. L42 —6C 20
Wilton St. L44 —1F 11
Wimbledon St. L45 —6F 3
Wimborne Av. L61 —4C 24
Wimborne Way. L61 —2H 23
Wimbrick Clo. L46 —5F 9
Wimbrick Hey. L46 —5F 9
Winchester Av. L65 —3B 48
Winchester Dri. L44 —1D 10
Windermere Clo. L64 —6D 36
Windermere Rd. L43 —2A 18
Windermere Rd. L65 —6D 48
Windfield Gdns. L66 —6D 40
Windle Ct. L64 —3C 36
Windmill Gdns. L43 —5A 10
Windsor Clo. L49 —4D 16
Windsor Clo. L62 —2G 27
Windsor Dri. L46 —6G 47
Windsor Rd. L45 —2F 3
Windsor St. L8 —6G 13
Windsor St. L41 —2G 19
Windways. L66 —6D 40
Windy Bank. L62 —3G 27
Winford St. L44 —2H 11
Winfrith Clo. L63 —1F 33
Winfrith Dri. L63 —1F 33

Wingate Clo. L43 —3C 18
Wingate Rd. L62 —6C 34
Winkle St. L8 —2H 21
Winnington Rd. L47 —3C 14
Winnington Rd. L48 —3C 14
Winser St. L62 —3H 27
Winsford Gro. L66 —4C 46
Winslow St. L4 —2H 5
Winstanley Rd. L62 —2H 27
Winston Dri. L43 —2A 18
Winston Gro. L46 —5E 9
Winter Gdns., The. L45 —3E 3
(off Atherton St.)
Winterhey Av. L44 —2F 11
Winter St. L6 —2H 13
Winthrop Pk. L43 —2C 18
Winton Clo. L45 —3D 2
Wirral Bus. Cen. L41 —3G 11
Wirral Bus. Pk. L49 —4F 17
Wirral Clo. L63 —6F 27
Wirral Cres. L64 —2D 42
Wirral Gdns. L63 —6F 27
Wirral Mt. L45 —6D 2
Wirral Mt. L48 —5F 15
Wirral Vs. L45 —5C 2
Wirral Way. L43 —2A 18
Wirral Way. L60 —3H 29
Withburn Clo. L49 —2E 17
Withensfield. L45 —5F 3
Withens La. L45 & L44 —5F 3
Withert Av. L63 —1D 26
Withington Rd. L44 —2G 11
Witley Av. L46 —4E 9
Witley Clo. L46 —4E 9
Witney Clo. L49 —4C 16
Wittenham Clo. L49 —3F 17
Wittering La. L60 —3H 29
Witterings, The. L64 —4C 36
Woburn Pl. L42 —5B 20
Woburn Rd. L45 —5F 3
Wolferton Clo. L49 —6H 9
Wolfe St. L8 —2G 21
Wolfrick Dri. L63 —2H 33
Wolsey St. L20 —2E 5
Wolstenholme Sq. L1 —5F 13
Wolverham Rd. L65 —4A 48
Woodacre Gro. L66 —5F 41
Woodacre Rd. L66 —5E 41
Woodbank Pk. L43 —3C 18
Woodbank Rd. L65 —5H 47
Woodberry Clo. L43 —3B 18
Woodbine St. L5 —4F 5
Woodburn Boulevd. L63
　—1E 27
Woodburn Dri. L60 —5B 30
Woodchurch Ct. L42 —4G 19
Woodchurch La. L42 —5F 19
Woodchurch La. L49 —1E 25
Woodchurch La. L66 —1E 47
Woodchurch Rd. L49, L43 &
　L41 —6H 17
Wood Clo. L41 —6H 11
Wood Clo. L66 —4A 40
Woodcote Av. L65 —5H 47
Woodcote Bank. L42 —6G 27
Woodcotes, The. L62 —5B 34
Woodcot La. L60 —2A 30
Woodcroft Dri. L61 —1B 30
Woodcroft La. L63 —1F 27
Woodend. L61 —4B 24
Wood End La. L64 —3A 44

Woodend Rd. L65 —1F 47
Woodfall Clo. L64 —1E 43
Woodfall Gro. L64 —1E 43
Woodfall La. L64 —1D 42
Woodfield Av. L63 —1F 27
Woodfield Rd. L61 —5A 24
Woodfield Rd. L63 —6G 27
Woodfield Rd. L65 —2A 48
Woodfield Rd. N. L65 —2A 48
Woodford Rd. L62 —1H 27
Wood Grn. L43 —5A 10
Woodhall Av. L44 —1H 11
Woodham Gro. L64 —2D 42
Woodhead Rd. L62 —3A 28
Woodhead St. L62 —2H 27
Woodhey Ct. L63 —1F 27
Woodhey Gro. L63 —2F 27
Woodhey Rd. L63 —2F 27
Woodhill. L49 —3H 17
Woodhouse Clo. L4 —4G 5
Woodin Rd. L42 —1E 41
Woodkind Hey. L63 —1G 33
Woodland Av. L47 —4F 7
Woodland Dri. L45 —4G 3
Woodland Dri. L49 —4G 17
Woodland Gro. L42 —1F 27
Woodland Rd. L42 —1F 27
Woodland Rd. L48 —5G 15
Woodland Rd. L49 —4G 17
Woodland Rd. L65 —5G 47
Woodlands Clo. L64 —5B 36
Woodlands Dri. L61 —5E 25
Woodlands Rd. L61 —4H 23
Woodlands Rd. L64 —5B 36
Woodlands, The. L41 —2H 19
Woodlands, The. L47 —1F 17
Woodland View. L66 —5B 40
Woodland Wlk. L62 —2A 34
Wood La. L45 —5C 2
Wood La. L49 —2D 16
Wood La. L64 —5G 43
(Burton)
Wood La. L64 —2A 36
(Parkgate)
Wood La. L64 —4C 38
(Willaston)
Woodlea Clo. L62 —6B 34
Woodpecker Clo. L49 —2D 16
Woodruff St. L8 —3H 21
Woodside. L65 —5A 48
Woodside Av. L46 —6D 8
Woodside Bus. Pk. L41 —6B 12
Woodside Ferry. L41 —6B 12
Woodside Ferry App. L41
　—6B 12
Woodside Rd. L61 —3A 24
Woodsome Clo. L66 —6H 47
Woodsome Dri. L65 —6G 47
Woodsorrel Rd. L41 —6D 10
Woodstock Rd. L44 —2E 11
Woodstock St. L5 —6F 5
Wood St. L1 —4F 13
Wood St. L41 —6H 11
Wood St. L47 —6D 6
Wood St. L62 —4H 27
Woodvale Clo. L43 —5A 10
Woodvale Ct. L49 —6H 17
Woodvale Rd. L66 —1D 46
Woodview Av. L44 —3H 11
Woodview Rd. L42 —3G 19
Woodward Rd. L42 —1G 27

Woodway. L49 —3E 17
Woodyear Rd. L62 —4C 34
Wooler Clo. L46 —5C 8
Woollam Rd. L66 —6D 40
Woolton Ct. L66 —5F 41
Worcester Ct. L20 —1F 5
Worcester Rd. L43 —5B 10
Worcester Rd. L65 —1A 48
Worcester Wlk. L65 —1A 48
Wordsworth Av. L42 —6B 20
Wordsworth Wlk. L48 —1A 22
Wordsworth Way. L66 —6E 47
Worthington St. L8 —1F 21
Wrenbury Clo. L43 —5D 18
Wrexham St. L5 —5F 5
Wright St. L5 —6F 5
Wright St. L44 —1H 11
Wroxham Clo. L49 —3G 17
Wroxham Ct. L49 —3G 17
Wroxham Dri. L49 —3G 17
Wroxham Way. L49 —3G 17
Wrynose Rd. L62 —3C 34
Wulstan St. L4 —4F 5
Wycherley Rd. L42 —4H 19
Wycliffe Rd. L6 —4F 47
Wycliffe St. L42 —5B 20
Wye Clo. L42 —4B 20
Wyedale. L65 —4H 47
Wye St. L5 —5H 5
Wykeham St. L4 —3F 5
Wykeham Way. L4 —4F 5
Wyncroft Clo. L66 —4H 47
Wyncroft St. L8 —3H 21
Wyndham Cres. L66 —5E 47
Wyndham Rd. L45 —6B 2
Wyndham St. L4 —1H 5
Wynstanley Rd. L64 —2C 42
Wynstay Rd. L47 —4E 7
Wyre Rd. L5 —4H 5
Wyvern Rd. L46 —5E 9

Yardley Dri. L63 —2G 33
Yates St. L8 —2G 21
Yates Wlk. L8 —2G 21
Yelverton Rd. L42 —4A 20
Yeoman Cotts. L47 —1E 15
Yeoman Way. L66 —6E 47
Yewdale Dri. L66 —6F 47
Yewdale Pk. L43 —4F 19
Yew Tree Clo. L49 —5G 17
Yewtree Clo. L64 —6D 36
Yewtree La. L48 —4D 14
Yew Tree Rd. L43 —3F 9
Yew Tree Rd. L63 —5E 27
Yew Way. L46 —4F 9
York Av. L44 —2H 11
York Av. L48 —6D 14
York Av. L44 —3H 11
York Rd. L45 —2A 48
York St. L1 —5F 13
York St. L9 —1H 5
York St. L62 —4B 28
York Ter. L5 —5G 5

Zetland Rd. L45 —4D 2
Zig Zag Rd. L45 —5F 3